THE PLOUGH AND THE PEN

The Plough and the Pen

WRITINGS FROM HUNGARY
1930–1956

EDITED BY
ILONA DUCZYŃSKA
AND KARL POLANYI

With a Foreword by W. H. Auden

McClelland and Stewart Limited

IN MEMORIAM
Endre Havas

Contents

CONTENTS

APPENDIX

Acknowledgments

The English versions of Tibor Déry's *Odysseus*, Gyula Illyés' *Ode to Bartók* and Lajos Tamási's *A Rhapsody on Truth as yet unformed* appeared first in *The New Reasoner;* of Áron Tamási's *Orderly Resurrection*, in *The New Hungarian Quarterly*; of Attila József's *Five Poor Men Speak* in *The Canadian Forum* and in *Ice Cod Bell or Stone* by Earle Birney, (McClelland and Stewart, Toronto, 1962); of Zoltán Zelk's *When I was a Thrush* and Ferenc Juhász' *At twenty-six* in *Collected Poems* by A. J. M. Smith, (Oxford University Press, Toronto, 1962).

Foreword

Ilona Duczyńska's prefatory essay on the historical background of the Hungarian writers represented in this anthology, and the biographical information contained in the appendix, leaves me with little to say but generalities.

One of the most striking characteristics of all forms of modern totalitarian régimes, one which enables us to distinguish them from traditional tyranny, is the political importance they attach to the arts. The traditional tyrant censored or suppressed works which were openly critical of and hostile to his tyranny, but artists whose work was without overt political content were unmolested and sometimes, even, encouraged. To the totalitarian movements of this century, on the other hand, there is something intrinsically politically dangerous in the process of artistic creation itself, irrespective of its subject matter. I do not think, for example, that either Hitler or Stalin had any illusions about the artistic quality of the literature which was produced to their specifications; that it should be worthless was precisely what they intended. Both recognised moreover that there is something dangerous about language itself and tried to create a pseudo-German and pseudo-Russian in which it would be impossible to make genuine statements about anything.

This was intelligent of them. Human beings acquired speech, not for practical purposes – for those the code-signals of animals would have sufficed – but in order to disclose themselves to each other. I can lie successfully to others so long as I am not really speaking in the first person singular. I can lie, that is to say, about matters of impersonal fact; for example, I can tell someone who has never visited the United States that there are no Chinese laundrymen in New York. I can also lie about my own past and say 'I went to Baltimore yesterday' when, in fact, I went to Boston, because my past is already outside myself and I can look at it as if it were someone else's. In such cases, though I may succeed in deceiving others, I cannot help knowing that I am telling a lie. I can, of course, choose to avoid learning certain facts because I am afraid of the truth and prefer to remain in ignorance, as the average German under Hitler, though he knew that concentration camps existed, preferred not to think about them.

On the other hand, when I really speak or write in the first person about what I am thinking and feeling, I may deceive myself, be perfectly convinced that I am telling the truth, but I can never deceive others. My language, my tone of voice will give me away. My listeners or readers may not be able to guess my real thoughts and feelings, but they will always know that these are not what I say they are.

All art, verbal, visual or musical, is personal utterance. Either it is genuine or it is bad, that is to say, not art at all, and we can only mistake it for art if we wish to be taken in.

We must not, of course, imagine that political freedom in itself guarantees the creation of good art; indeed one of the most obvious characteristics of any country where there is freedom of speech and publication is the vast quantity of rubbish which gets spoken and printed. Persons with a love of truth and a talent to perceive and utter it are, unfortunately, a minority, but only under conditions of freedom can this minority develop its powers and have an influence.

I have had to listen in my life to many discussions of the role of the artist in society and very boring and fruitless they all were. Every writer has, of course, certain social and political duties and responsibilities as a citizen like other citizens: what these are will depend upon the age and society in which he happens to be living. But the only political duty – by duty I mean an activity which takes up time which he might prefer to devote to his own writing – which I can see as falling on a writer, in all countries and at all times, his duty, not as a citizen but as a person with literary talent, is a duty to translate the fiction and poetry of other countries so as to make them available to readers in his own. I consider translation a political act because the relations between any two countries are not determined by economic and political interests alone, but also by the degree to which the inhabitants of each are able to understand what the inhabitants of the other are thinking and feeling, and the novelists and poets of a country are the only people who can give one this understanding. The compilers and translators of this anthology have done something for Canada, the United States, England and Hungary which no tourist bureau or 'engaged' journalist could possibly have done.

This is not the place for a critical article about the prose and poetry of modern Hungary. Aside from its literary merits, it cannot fail to interest an English, American or Canadian reader, because the kind of life and experiences which it portrays are so different from our own. None of us has lived, either as a landlord or as a peasant, in a semi-feudal agricultural society; the kinds of social cruelty and injustice with which we are familiar, those of industrialism, are absent here.

Nor have we known what it is like to live under a police terror in which people are tempted for the safety of themselves and their family to denounce their friends. The Iron Curtain, the Cold War, may be facts of our time, but let us beware of acquiring an Iron-Curtain mentality which equates good and evil with our respective political and economic structures. The criticism, overt or covert, of life in Hungary both before and after World War Two which many of these writers express does not mean that they would prefer to live in the United States any more than the criticism of American capitalism implied by the character of Babbit means that Sinclair Lewis would have preferred to live in Russia.

As to their literary merit, the reader can decide for himself. I should like to say, however, that, though I do not know a word of Hungarian and though no translation can ever do justice to a poem, I am convinced that *The Boy Changed into a Stag Cries out at the Gate of Secrets* by Ferenc Juhász is one of the greatest poems written in my time.

W.H.A.

Preface

The prose and verse from Hungary which this volume contains were written between the 1930's and the October Rising of 1956.

Movements that do not achieve their immediate objectives may still leave a momentous imprint that only time reveals. The Hungarian Revolt was seeking a union of freedom and socialism: that was the secret of its power and passion. The writers and poets of 1956 did not, for the sake of an idea of abstract freedom, abandon socialism's work-in-progress, insincere and morally corroded as it had grown to be. Their answer to the dilemma of the age was to stake their lives on their personal integrity. To stand for truth became in their eyes the supreme need in building a new society. This act of maturity was understood by the country, and to some extent, the world.

We have named this book *The Plough and the Pen* in honour of the Hungarian Populists. Little known outside Hungary, this movement, along with the Communist party reformers played an incisive role in the rebirth of 1956. The two together gave a lead to all the persuasions in Hungarian literature, united in their resistance to the regime's literary policy.

Populist beginnings lie back in the early Thirties, when first a stir was felt, coming from the peasant intelligentsia. Young people of peasant origin advocated a radical land reform. The Populists developed the new discipline of rural sociology; their novelists delved into the history of forgotten regions and social strata; their thinkers, breaking with a feudalist tradition, posited the landless millions as the body of the nation. Practical advances in agriculture, communal living and education, which they initiated, brought about a cultural rejuvenation in the desolate countryside. A spirit of democratic resistance spread among the poorest peasantry. The new force came to be known as the Populist movement, which at the end of the Thirties organized as the National Peasant Party.

By 1945, when, with the Russian sponsored coalition government, political life came to the surface and open intellectual contest started, the Populists were a factor on the Left, but were subsequently eclipsed in the villages by Communist militancy. Ten years later a bureaucratic Communist Party collapsed, leaving a void in place of the revolutionary establishment. In the total crisis the

empirical bent that inhered in Populism came to life, giving re-
newed content to nationhood.

The book contains works of the Populist writers and of the
Communist party reformers.

Part One consists of prose on three themes.

The first of these, *Waste Land*, brings writings of the inter-war
years. With sombre passion they tell of a Hungary ruined and
degraded by the landowning class. To abolish the latifundia was
the foremost need of social change in Hungary.

The next, *Pinions of Poverty*, contains prose written after 1945.
It is full of hope. It recounts the partitioning of the land; the first
steps – tentative but voluntary – in the setting up of a collective
farm; the salvaging of a human wreck in a factory.

The last, *Pledge*, is work written around 1956. The tragedy of
the fake trial against Rajk, carried out on Stalin's orders, had
undermined the country's morale. Government had turned into
tyranny. But an integrity, that transcends the tragic, replied in
the voices of Déry, the Communist, and Németh, the non-Communist, with a pledge to all that is indestructible in man: to personal
relationships; and to truth, even though man in his fallen condition
had already denied it.

Part Two of the volume presents poetry.

History moved fast in '56. The poet laid bare 'the good, the vile,
the saving grace, the sin'. On a smaller scale Stalin's crimes were
duplicated in Hungary by Rákosi. Communists and Socialists
disappeared in the prisons and in mass graves, dishonoured and
forsaken by their closest friends who had believed the charges
against them. In the sudden flash of realization the Communist
poets bore witness to their remorse. They re-dedicated themselves
to truth, to the freedom of creative expression, to their disinherited
nation.

The editors of this selection, Ilona Duczyńska and Karl Polanyi,
have lived away from their Hungarian homeland for over forty
years and their respective activities in Budapest had faded for
them to memories. It was during the war, in 1943, that they joined
the movement of Michael Károlyi, in his London exile. The
distribution of land in 1945 brought the hope of a Hungarian
revival. In the Summer of 1948 I.D. travelled in the countryside
of her youth, retracing the steps of the Populist village explorers
and studying the results of the land reform.

This book of homage is the fruit of their several pasts and their long converging lives.

The Canadian poets responded to the self-imposed silence of the poets of Hungary. Setting aside what may have divided them in aesthetics and philosophy, they rendered into English a selection of contemporary Hungarian poetry.

To make the English versions of the poems, a number of aids were employed. Hungarian, its rhythms and its very idea of poetry were alien to the English-speaking poets. Bi-lingual 'red-and-black' work sheets were used, giving the literal translations and word identifications, the rhyme and assonance patterns, number of syllables and rhythmic pictures. Tape recordings as well as many verbal readings of the originals were needed and, most of all, close personal contact between the poet and the translator-interpreter.

Thanks are due to Canadian and English friends who helped at all stages in reading manuscripts and made much-valued contributions. Professor Kenneth Muir, of the University of Liverpool, made a final revision of some of the prose texts.

With the exception of Péter Veres' *The Test*, which was the work of Alexander Harsányi, Part One was translated by Ilona Duczyńska. Almost all the verbatim translations of the poetry were also done by her. The verbatim translations of some of the later poems by Ferenc Juhász were prepared by Karl Polanyi. The final selection of poems as they appear in this volume was influenced by circumstances beyond our control.

W. H. Auden most kindly read the verbatim 'red-and-black' translations of the poems and his encouragement over the years helped the editors to bear up against many difficulties.

Pickering, Ontario   I.D.
December, 1959   K.P.

The Hungarian Populists

AN INTRODUCTION

After the failure of the national rising of 1848, and the Compromise with victorious Austria twenty years later, Hungary found herself half-way towards becoming one of the modern nation-states of Europe. The rapidly forming middle class remained weak and alien. It was confined to Budapest and mainly consisted of industrious German artisans and the fast assimilating Jewish businessmen. The Magyar nobility refused to go into trade and held a monopoly of army commissions and administrative posts in government and county. The aristocracy, mostly alien, attached to the foreign dynasty, and holding immense landed property, went into high finance. A carry-over from serfdom existed side by side with an unbridled economic liberalism.

THE ANTECEDENTS

Around the turn of the century a grass-roots movement sprang up among the vast agricultural labour force of landless peasants, sharecroppers, itinerant harvest gangs, and even among the paid-in-kind estate servants, the *hacienda peons* of Hungary. It was savagely repressed by force of arms. By that time labour unions on the German social democratic model were well established in the metropolis. From the outset the land question was alien to them and the disastrous cleavage between rural and urban labour was widening. The rural paupers still had no place in the nation. The growth of industry, a Western cultural orientation and a general modernizing trend brought no change in the rural Waste Land.

In the early years of the century progressive thought penetrated deeply into the rising middle class and its complement of impoverished nobility – in short, the intelligentsia. It made a powerful impact. In literature and in the social sciences new ways opened up in opposition to the forces of the past that still ruled over the country. In the newly founded literary periodical *Nyugat* (Occident) a generation of writers found their home. Endre Ady's poetry brought a new era in literature, revolutionizing the language. The scholarly pursuits of the Sociological Society gave rise to men of Oscar Jászi's civic stature. He embodied a statesmanlike conception of democratic nationhood, with primacy of the peasant question and the rights of non-Magyar minorities. An earnest and idealistically-minded student movement, the Galileo Circle, prepared the underprivileged young intelligentsia for future leadership. The socialist working-class movement was gaining impetus.

But intellectual progressivism in the early 1900's, like the labour movement, resided in the capital city. Even home-town roots were severed. Sons of impoverished nobles from distant villages, sons of the small businessmen or professionals from rural towns found a longed-for refuge in the metropolitan wilderness and its world of *littérateurs*. And just as the literary revival of the *Nyugat* remained the intellectual climate of the educated only, progressive political thought, for all its awareness, failed to make the link with the social realities of a basically peasant country. This fateful weakness was the undoing of two revolutions: both the progressive middle class in 1918, and, after them, the revolutionary working class in 1919 were unable to win the support of the peasantry and bring them onto the historical stage. Yet nothing short of a human reconstruction could have created a democratic nation strong enough to stay the onslaught of the counter-revolution. The revolution of 1918 was merely the fruit of defeat and lacked a social programme, despite the initiative of Count Michael Károlyi, who distributed his own lands among the landless. The Communists, in 1919, failed to distribute the big landed estates among the pauperized peasantry. They ousted the big landowners and ran the estates as public property. After their fall and the return to power of the landlord class, the counter-revolutionary régime of Admiral Horthy took cruel vengeance on the villagers and agricultural labourers who were said to have taken part in running the domains. Thus, on the one hand, the rural poor had not received the land, and on the other, they were victimized as though they had. More than ever before distrust and apathy gripped them.

The counter-revolution consolidated its hold. Disillusionment with liberalism and reform, with socialism and democracy was general after the abortive revolutions of 1918 and 1919. The country lay wide open to fascist indoctrination – which flourished in native variants as well as in the German version at a later date.

Organized labour received during the 'twenties a modicum of legal recognition on condition that it renounce the right to organize rural labour. Under the impact of the world economic crises at the beginning of the 'thirties the pauperization of the countryside reached its peak. The landless peasantry and their families now numbered one in every three inhabitants of the small country. These were Hungary's 'three million beggars'.

POPULIST ORIGINS

Contrasting with the gloom that hung over Hungary, a creative influence began to make itself felt towards the end of the 'twenties, which, within a short period, was to broaden out into a veritable cultural revolution. From the outset it was more than a movement. Spurred by the unspeakable conditions among the agro-proletarian population, young writers, scholars, students answered the challenge and began to investigate matters on their own, and to describe them. It was not an urge to 'go among the people', *v narod*, as the Russian intelligentsia felt it in the later nineteenth century. The Hungarians, on the contrary, had come out of the people. They were an intelligentsia of peasant stock, who now turned homeward in anger for a thorough insight and a bitter summing up. The task was immense, and it so happened that it found the country's supreme talent at its service. Following in the footsteps of Bartók and Kodály and transplanting their revolutionary methods from music to the world of letters, they found in the untouched layers of the people's ways and language the art of modern expression, an art that abhorred the sentimental, the romantic, the 'folksy'. Their aims were high. The impact on the country was tremendous.

The Populist writers, as they later were called, differed much among themselves in thought, method, expression and temperament. There was no common doctrine. What they had in common was creative freedom and a sense of anger. The Populist *oeuvre* consisted of some four or five dozen books – close-ups of peasant life, regional sociographies, novels, ethnographic studies, poems, statistics, diaries, family histories and minute descriptions of single villages. The poet Gyula Illyés, in 1933, called upon the youth 'to explore the village'. Earnest young scholars tramped along the dusty expanse of the Great Plain. Poets dedicated themselves to the humble, painstaking tasks of rural sociography.

In the mid 'thirties Gyula Illyés wrote his largely autobiographical *People of the Puszta*, opening up a submerged world. Péter Veres, himself a landless peasant, wrote his *Village Chronicle;* Zoltán Szabó his pioneering village study, *The Situation at Tard;* József Darvas his *History of a peasant family;* Imre Kovács his indictment of the Horthy régime; Ferenc Erdei, a peasant's son, his erudite regional studies; János Kodolányi his sombre demographic pictures; Géza Féja his study of Southern Hungary.

Áron Tamási produced his peasant myths and parables; László Németh, the novelist and playwright, his multifarious ideas on communal rural existence. After 1945 the group suffered a few losses on the fringes. József Darvas became a Communist; Imre Kovács and Zoltán Szabó who were abroad, eventually sided with Western policies. None of the Populist writers left Hungary in 1956.

Their works were variations on a common theme. The Populist writers were searching for the mainsprings of peasant society. There, if anywhere, lay the potential nation in its vigour – elusive, recondite. The immediate purpose was undoubtedly to probe into the ills of the peasantry, to expose the corroding effects of their landless existence, and the deformation of life that is brought on by despair. But as the total work took shape, it brought more than that. It entailed a realization of the cultural manifold of the rural population, of the sharply delineated regions and the varied imprints left on them by history.

Social doctrines and social myths were equally discounted, out of the conviction that to record truly you must approach reality with a blank sheet. The spectrum of opinions ranged from class struggle to nativism in many hues. The equalitarian trend dominated and the peasant's claim to land was the prime motive with all the Populists. Marxism as such had remained outside the experience of their generation. Politically, the Populists brought back to life the rural radicalism of the turn of the century. In the course of their explorations a distinct policy emerged: complete partitioning of the big landed estates among the landless, in order to strip the squire of all inherited prestige; consolidation of holdings, to raise agricultural productivity; and a plan for resettlement to overcome a ruthless and cruel practice of abortion which prevented the birth of more than one child to a family in certain regions.

Within a span of three or four years the inert country was roused. Many of the ruling class were conscience-stricken. The village exploring movement had brought new life to a despairing people. The reports found their way back to the very nooks and crannies of villages, farmsteads and *pusztas*, whence they had sprung. By the end of the 'thirties the Populist writers had become the vehicle of the aspirations of landless peasants and agro-proletarians. They made themselves their political exponents: in 1937 the March Front was founded and, in a historic conference held upon a raft on the River Maros in 1939 its successor, the National Peasant

Party. It faced up boldly to the persecutions of the Horthy régime and united the country's best writers with her poorest peasants. It was a prophetic combination.

An episode of that time, later to gain great significance, was the publication in 1938 of a book on Marxism and Populism under an assumed name. It was reprinted in 1946 over the signature of its author, József Révai, a high ranking Marxist critic and brilliant pupil of György Lukács. It tried to reconcile the two leftist camps, and asserted that Populist sociography represented the most significant trend of thought the country had known in twenty years; Marxists had much to learn from it.

PARTITIONING OF THE LANDED ESTATES

In the event, the Hungarian peasants did not receive their land as the result of any great struggle, nor through any initiative of their own, but by the Red Army's victorious advance. In the Autumn of 1944 the Soviet armoured divisions, sweeping Hitler's armies before them, entered the Hungarian Plain from the southeast. The landed gentry and the rural middle classes were on the run, trekking behind the retreating German Army. An amorphous mass of peasants, industrial workers, artisans and shopkeepers stayed on. Local administration had dissolved.

In the wake of their progress the Soviet military authorities launched a partitioning of the great estates. They set up local claimants' committees. Nothing could have been more appropriate. Hungary in 1945 was a country of which one third of the entire population was formed of people who possessed no land at all, who were mere hired workers on the estates, seasonal or casual labourers, along with the rural paupers who lived on starvation plots.

The peasants, however, were too far gone to take matters readily into their own hands. At first it seemed that nothing would shake their lethargy deepened by fear, suspense and the heavy losses in Hitler's war. In vain did circumstance offer them the land they had dreamt of, it had a taste of unreality. The fortunes of war, after all, might turn and bloody vengeance fall upon them, as after the revolution of 1919. The chances of a total break with the past were regarded with disbelief. The outlook did not altogether change even when, under the new government, in the spring of 1945 the radical land reform was to start in all parts of the country. The peasants only awoke in the very shock of performing the historic act. The evil of a thousand years was discarded at the rate of a century a day over a period of roughly ten days – the length of time it took in most villages to carry out the partitioning of the land.

The land reform sponsored by the Russians in effect incorporated ideas and suggestions of the Populist writers and rural sociologists, whose recommendations had been more radical than the ones put forward by the Hungarian Communists. In later years, as converts to Communism, the Populists' intense loyalty rested on the fact that the perennial longing of the poor peasant had been fulfilled by Soviet Communism. The land reform was the great divide between the old Hungary and the new. None of the later developments was of the same order of magnitude. The years that brought iniquity and misgovernment, forced collectivization and grain deliveries at nominal prices were a blight on the land reform, not its undoing. The utter expropriation of the big landowners proved unshakeable and irreversible. There was no *La Vendée* in Hungary. In 1956 the peasants destroyed any hopes the *ancien régime* may have nursed of using the rising as a means of its own return. The peasants stood firmly against the former landlords: they carted free food to the striking factory workers, and held on to the land. Some time after 1956 extensive collectivization created a new and as yet unsolved agrarian problem.

The New Village: Populists and Communists

While the land reform itself was not the peasants' own achievement, the settlement of the new lands was. Animals and machinery were lacking. The new peasant farms were successfully established in the devastated country at the cost of a supreme effort and much personal sacrifice. The new holdings took root, and after a few harvests the fear of a return of the landlords faded.

At this time two parties existed in the villages as closely-knit organized bodies, the National Peasant Party of the Populists and the Communist Party. Both represented the poor peasantry, the new holders of land. The powerful and numerous Smallholders' Party had a more indefinite character – it was a large body of voters and represented the non-expropriated, better-off peasants. It was, at the same time likely to attract the expropriated classes and their supporters: a counter-revolutionary party inside the ruling coalition.

In the eyes of the West the Populists' National Peasant Party appeared as the usual crypto-Communist grouping. As a matter of fact, the two parties were bitter rivals contending for the new peasantry whom they both genuinely represented. There was a deep difference in temper, tradition and modes of action, a difference which later proved decisive. The Peasant Party acknowledged the 'natural hierarchy' of the village, although they, too, drew the line at the wealthy peasant who was, of course, an employer of agricultural labour. The Communist Party, on the other hand, disrupted the intricate social structure of the village. The communities in which they shared in the administration were unquiet and tense, as the half-Catholic, half-Calvinist towns and villages of the Great Plain had traditionally been. More often entire villages were either Communist run or Peasant Party run. In regions where modern business methods had been developed on the former great estates, the Communists held sway; where life was moving in more traditional grooves, the Populists ruled. Even the type of village leaders were different – dynamic, burly personalities on the Communist side, against the contemplative Peasant Party men, either peasants or peasant-minded intellectuals, usually well acquainted with the eminently readable Populist literature.

THE CULTURAL SCENE

The difference in the two radical parties' climate of opinion, background and ethics showed very clearly in the youth of the grammar schools and universities. The students of the Györffy College, a group of ethnographers and rural sociologists, had been heroes of the resistance against the Nazis. After 1945 they became the young people's idols. The Populist writings, by this time classics, acted as a powerful leaven. Deeply influenced by this heritage, young people banded together to emulate the Györffy College, improvising a settlement, a 'People's College' in some abandoned half-ruined house with just a few sacks of beans and flour, given in their support by Populist sympathizers. The country was still in ruins. People's Colleges were soon attached to almost every grammar school, technical school, art school, music school, and the various Departments of the Universities. They were a grass-roots movement, creating close communities of students, homes of discussion and free growth, of personal friendship and achievement. In brief, centres of future leadership. The movement spread as it had sprung up, not started by any single act and controlled by none. The People's Colleges later founded a Federation, which became in course of time a veritable battleground between the contending ideologies. The Populist-inspired young people were seekers, with a deep-rooted conviction that answers should be found empirically and would work themselves out. The Communist complement among the student leaders were seminar-trained, knowing all the answers.

By 1948 the Populist youth began to accept Communist doctrine. Not, at that time, under compulsion, but swayed by what appeared as the inescapable logic of history. The recalcitrant remnant was swept away by administrative methods. The Colleges, taken over by the Communists, soon lost their distinctive character.

But it was the Populist converts to Communism who were to write an unexpected chapter in history. After almost ten years the original inspiration of their thought and method was to come to the surface in 1956 from beneath the overlay of Communist doctrine. In the year '56, converts were reconverted to the beliefs of their youth, and veteran Communists now joined hands with them. The former inmates of the People's Colleges, now in their early thirties, gave leadership to the Petőfi Circle.

Lukács and the Literary Debate

In 1945 the Populist writers, mostly in their forties, were at the peak of their creative power. Their writing had matured. Their thought broadened and branched out into differing persuasions. How would Marxism affect them? How would they affect Marxism? The question was crucial.

These were the candid years. The Left of every shade and opinion moved in a climate of freedom it had never known. Formerly this had been the privilege of the Right. If this privilege was now somewhat curtailed, the Right was still able to make the most of it by sheer force of historical routine: revolutions in Hungary, in their experience, were to be regarded as something transitory and doomed to fail. The quarter century of ultranationalist, full-blooded fascist indoctrination died hard and provided a popular following for the dispossessed 'historical classes' who were biding their time. The Left had many shades, yet one common revolutionary purpose: to destroy the *ancien régime* – that feudal past and its modern bastard out of *laissez-faire* capitalism. In doing so the Left gained considerable strength.

The political tensions between Left and Right grew with every new achievement in the country's reconstruction and social liberation. On the Left, controversy about the role and future of democracy was vigorous. Whether the democratic freedom of the first three years was foredoomed, is debatable. It was real while it lasted. The cleavage between the ultimate perspectives of the revolutionary parties themselves threatened to rend the revolution. And literature was fated to be the main battlefield.

György Lukács, the Marxist philosopher of world fame and leading critic in literature turned with sympathetic interest towards the Populist writers. He combined high-level Marxist thinking with an endeavour to create a platform for a broad liberalism in matters of literature. This brand of Marxist liberalism was entirely unknown in the Communist world. Lukács supported it with an original view of the relations between literature and society, and between literature and history – a system of thought which was in the last resort based on the humanist component in Karl Marx' philosophy. His aesthetics allowed him an elasticity otherwise foreign to a doctrinaire outlook whether in politics, religion or art. Great artists, he thought, may create immortal masterpieces, while holding an entirely false philosophy. The good cause may benefit by cultural achievements not only different from, but even hostile to, one another. Both Slavophils and Westerners, he argued, served the Russian freedom movement of the nineteenth century. When there is an underlying unity of purpose, when a whole people is on the move for its liberation, the backwash will make the writers of the time serve the cause of emancipation, no matter how much they differ in general outlook.

Lukács' dream of sheltered islands of freedom within the onrush of a social revolution was, in the circumstances, bound to fail. He succeeded particularly in winning over to Communism the young Populist intelligentsia. But Communism was in an increasingly doctrinaire phase. Soon the youth itself turned against his liberal ideas and sided with the rigid party line on literature as on all else.

The new tensions of social transformation now pervaded the whole of society, imposing their alternatives on life issues. The youth became restive, assailed by genuine doubt as to whether the emotional traditionalism, the diffuse inspirations and contradictory utopias on which they grew up actually offered a way into the future. They veered round towards the more radical solutions of the Communist policies with the zeal of the convert: Let the country, at long last, be built up on new foundations, in a new framework: Militancy first! Their need was not for Tolstoi and Balzac. If they were to bear the brunt of socialist construction, literature had to depict the heroic aspects of their own everyday lives. It was a case for what is known as 'socialist realism'. *Inter arma silent musae.*

Many young converts of 1948 burned their bridges, leaving behind what made them. Young historians and sociologists threw out their entire libraries. Sociography was dropped. It had acquired in their eyes a counter-revolutionary connotation.

Unbelievable though it seemed to the world, young poets had willingly endorsed the principle of literary regimentation.

In the retrospect of ten years one of their generation described this shift: 'In our surpassing certitude we hardly realized, that sometime around 1948 our attention began to wander from the realities of life as it was building up around us, and began to take its bearings *solely and exclusively*, and with mounting passion on constructing the ideological framework . . . We swore by the People, the Workers, the Peasants, yet our eardrums did not sense their heavy breathing, a rosy mist shrouded our eyes, blinded to the agony and distress of the lives around . . .'.*

In 1949 the blow fell. The party philosopher Rudas launched a personal attack on Lukács. He called for the suppression of all but socialist realist literature. Zhdanov's doctrine became the literary policy in Hungary. Lukács recanted. Early in 1950 he withdrew into academic life.

Only in the summer of '56 did the youth turn again towards the humanist vision that Lukács had courageously sustained for so long.

ZHDANOV AND THE FIRST SILENCE

After Lukács' defeat almost all the writers who held first place in Hungarian letters were silenced. The works of the village explorers were taken out of circulation and banned. The monthly *Válasz* (The Answer), edited by Gyula Illyés, was suppressed, though Illyés' poetry continued to be published. László Németh by 1948 had concluded the novel, named after its heroine, *Égető Eszter*, a Wilhelm Meister of his time. It remained unpublished until 1956–57. The story of Áron Tamási's childhood, *Cradle and Owl*, remained unprinted, as did also the manuscripts of Féja and Kodolányi, who always had strong national affinities; of the veteran Socialist and working-class poet Kassák, who still wrote in Whitmanic verse; the 'urbanist' poet-writer Milán Füst; the poet Lőrinc Szabó, whose lyricism was purely personal, and many others. They withdrew from the nation's view, eking out life as translators, tutors, village librarians, eventually going back home, if there happened to be some outlying farm building to go to.

* Sándor Erdei in *Kortárs* (Budapest) No. 1, 1958, p.107.

They were keyed up for ultimate effort. The creative vein did not give out. Their writings were stored. The silence lasted seven years with interruptions; in 1953 and '54 a thaw set in under Imre Nagy, regimentation returned again in 1955 with Rákosi and broke only in 1956.

The literary harvest of the writers' First Silence, when it was published, overwhelmed and enraptured the country.

While these works were written in poverty and oblivion, the approved writers worked in bodily comfort under public surveillance. Open governmental concern with work-in-progress, its occasional public discussion, not stopping short of express guidance and textual corrections, must have been irksome enough even to the writer who was in harmony with his undertaking, sitting in a glass house and having a searchlight playing on his writing desk. In the years of doubt such interference became a nightmare, an onslaught on the writer's integrity. The required works were written. They were processed; they did not ring true.

In 1952 a public discussion of the works of thirty prominent writers was held. József Révai had lately become the protagonist of 'socialist realism' and the literary dictator of Hungary. He attacked Tibor Déry a dedicated Communist, and the hero of his partly-written trilogy, *Response*. Déry's pure in heart adolescent worker was denounced as the product of 'petty bourgeois moralism'. The attack misfired. The ideological terror, now at its peak, left the writers frustrated and confused.

The Postulate of Truth

Between 1953 and 1955 Imre Nagy had fought a losing battle on the governmental plane, although he succeeded in having released and rehabilitated many innocent victims of the Stalin era. But he was countered by Rákosi, as General Secretary, who ousted him in a Stalinist restoration.

Rákosi did his worst to subdue the writers whose conscience had been roused. They fought back with the courage of despair, driven by a sickening consciousness of the tragic fate of their innocent comrades and the guilt they had been made to share. This deep unrest was spearheaded by the Communist writers and poets, and subsequently joined by every trend in Hungarian literature, including even those writers and journalists who shortly after the collapse crossed the border and threw in their lot with the political West.

Criticism was voiced by the Petőfi Circle – significantly intended first to be named after Galileo, as was the historic student circle, its forerunner half a century ago. Originally the Petőfi Circle had been an offshoot of the Communist youth organization with the purpose of relieving boredom by discussion. But with the growing insight into the party's depravity the membership broadened out to include Hungary's intellectuals – poets, writers, philosophers, economists, historians and social scientists.

Their discussions now belong to history. The interplay of Populist thought with the humanist aspect of Marxism resulted in a drive for party reform and the vision of a Hungary socialist in her own right.

In the grim days that followed the catastrophe, the nation lived on by the strength of its newly-won coherence, manifested in fearlessness and a continuing flow of cultural life. The complex picture resembled victory more than defeat.

THE SECOND SILENCE AND AFTER

The revival of letters in 1956 was not cut off by the cataclysmic months. The works that had matured during the first silence were still rolling off the printing press after October. The Populist classics, long out of print, were republished and filled the book-stalls. The country embraced its heritage. Németh's collected social dramas and historical plays were published in 1957. Also in the same year, in a class by itself, stood the publication of the collected poetic works of the young Ferenc Juhász, a landmark in Hungarian lyricism. Modern Western writing also began to be widely published.

At the same time new persecution had set in. A number of poets and writers, mostly Communists, suffered imprisonment for the part they had played in the sparking of the Revolt. Others, barred from writing, subsisted in obscurity. Yet others were being entreated by the government to publish their recent works. In solidarity with their persecuted friends and colleagues they withheld their voice: led by the poet Gyula Illyés they refused to have their newer writings published. A grand campaign, conducted 'against the so-called Populist writers' filled the literary monthlies, weeklies and even the reading supplements of the daily press for the length of one whole year – proof positive of their standing. The accused remained aloof. When the year was over the ineffectual discussion was called off. The writers' silence held as long as the prison doors remained closed. Illyés' verse began to appear again in April, 1960, when Tibor Déry and many others were released from captivity. Benjámin also published again in a new monthly *Uj Irás* (*New Writing*). Their poems are the country's bread and wine.

A new surge of talent has come – once again mostly out of peasant homes – in the persons of the youngest poets, among them Mihály Váci.

Literary policy by now is fairly attuned to an amount of freedom for the writer to write and for the public to read. Áron Tamási and László Németh, who hold the nation's confidence have assumed the playwright's supreme task, in drawing, with the good intent to heal, the candid picture of human affairs in present-day Hungary – Németh in his whimsical play *The journey*, Tamási in the deeper paradigm of his poetic comedy *The blissful aspen-leaf*. Populist thought, whose constructive powers stand tested in history and literature is proving a live force in Hungary.

Ilona Duczyńska

Part One

WASTE LAND

To Eat One's Fill

I

In the Jurassic Age the Magyar Plain lay at the bottom of the sea. Now in our time, this Age of Hunger, it is once more like a sea.

No hillock, no rise in any spot, flat earth encircled by the sky. The plain is so level, it might be the sea's surface, except that no sea has such rigidity. The wheat stands as evenly as though celestial engineers had traced out the height of each stalk with a ruler, so that not one would break the silky smoothness of the field.

The sky covers it like an upturned glass bowl on which playful angels are casting clouds and wonderful white and blue colours.

It seems as if the Count's domains are right in the middle of the world. Looking round, your eyes meet the rim of the sky, whichever way you turn under the 360 degrees of the circle.

The young lord, too, sees himself in the centre of the universe, for wherever he goes the labourers salute him on his thoroughbred as they would a young god passing by.

He now approaches a field, almost a mile square: a sugar beet plantation, an expanse so smooth that it makes you giddy. The young plants stand up like dainty little schoolgirls doing their gymnastic drill; whichever way one looks, the lines fan out and run on as straight as an arrow.

The young lord can see far afield from his mount, there's not a tree nor even a tuft of bush anywhere. From the saddle he towers above a world of minute plants. He scans the distances for the labour gang he is looking for, the one he sought out the day before, and the day before that, every day this week – and it's Friday afternoon now.

The labourers are in groups of seventies. Seventy men wielding the hoe, stooping over the beet, cutting away the weeds meticulously, earthing up a small cone-shaped mound for each plantlet in the immense field.

33

At last he catches sight of the group he is looking for and rides up to them along the path.

He gets there as it turns noon.

The foreman makes a sign and the labourers straighten up and stop hoeing. It is dinnertime; they step out of the row and make for the edge of the field where the wives and children are waiting for them with the food.

Although they have to carry it in pots from the village, yet the wives get there on the stroke of noon when the bells begin to peal in the distant spires.

The young lord dismounts and tosses the reins to a lad who rushes forward to catch them. He walks up to the foreman and asks him:

'Well, when will you have finished this patch?'

The Count is a sinewy young sportsman, of thirty. The foreman is a gloomy old man of sixty-five. The Count is gay and light-hearted; the old man is crooked-necked and crabbed.

He answers very humbly:

'Your lordship mustn't take it amiss, but the ground is exceedingly hard – it hasn't rained for a long time. We get along slowly, only the weeds grow fast. I don't see how we could finish this field by Saturday evening, not unless we kept hoeing all night.'

The Count does not care in the least. He has asked when they would finish merely to show he had a reason to be out in the fields.

He nods and says:

'Well, keep hoeing all night.'

The foreman scratches his head and says:

'Beg pardon, my lord, but the men couldn't be made to do that, not for all the wages Your Lordship was to offer.'

The Count laughs, looks round, and sees what he came for – a tall, slender young wife, she is just handing her husband the crock with the day's midday meal.

2

She also glances at the young lord, blushes a little, sways grace-fully, and then goes on as if she hadn't seen him at all.

She turns to her husband who is already squatting on the ground, and says:

'Eat, dear.'

'What have you got?' asks the man.

'What d'you think? A little soup. Same as yesterday.'

The man knows well there is nothing at home on the shelves. The pantry is bare. Sullenly, he reaches for the crock and takes it between his knees.

He lifts it out of the string bag in which the food was carried, and removes the lid from the crock. He peers in.

True enough, nothing is in it except the brownish slop. Small spots of grease, turned solid, float on top and the cold fat clings to the tin spoon as he dips it in.

He says nothing, for there is nothing he can say. There is bleak hunger in the villages. It had been a grim winter. They had run out of everything. What with last year's drought and the crops failing, they could not store any food for the winter. They are deep in debt. Even though work has started in the fields, wages are very poor, one pengö a day. Workers in far-away, happier lands would never believe that anyone could live on so little. Yet they even manage to pay off debts, and go without food like starving dogs. He must not take it out on his wife for having nothing better or more for him to eat, for it is to a woman's credit, when her man is uncomplaining . . . Wheat is low in price, and the manor cannot pay better wages, either.

He only sighs, and ladles a few spoonfuls of the thin broth. He even cheers up at the sight of a couple of dumplings he discovers in the pot. The woman made them of flour, and they float in the dark liquid like soft, primordial creatures.

The man's name is Kis. Kis János. He has the briefest name and the longest poverty. He trails his poverty as dusk trails the shadows, when they swoon away to the eastern fringes.

His face set, he begins to eat, with an effort. Always the same stuff. Soup in the morning, soup at midday, and when he gets home, soup again.

'To think of all the soup I have put away in my days', he says. 'Bucketfuls! Why, there isn't a barrel to hold it, even in the Archbishop's cellar.'

The woman keeps silent. Absent-mindly, she happens to look in the direction where the young lord is standing in talk with the men.

The labourers, however, are settled down apart, one here, the other there. They cover up the crocks in which their food was brought. The fare is poor for one and all, nothing to show off. They stoop over their earthenware pots and quietly ladle away.

'Did you bring any water?' asks Kis János.

'No, not today.'

35

'Why not?'

'You took some along in the morning, didn't you?'

'A quart. I took a quart, but it's gone.'

'Why did you drink it all?'

'Why did I drink it? Do I have to cut down on water now?'

The woman stands and ponders a while.

'I'd better be off and fetch you some.'

'Hurry up, then.'

The wife takes the quart bottle from his satchel. There's nothing in the satchel but a small piece of bread. She takes that out, too, and hands it to her man.

'Eat it.'

'Eat it? If I eat it, it's gone.'

'But you mustn't drop dead of hunger, either.'

'I mustn't? That's women's talk, they don't know the Army. In the ranks, when a man opened his last tin, they bound him leg to neck, and if it happened in battle he was shot. I'm saving my last piece of bread. Who knows? There'll be famine yet on the manor land.'

The wife is silent. With the bottle in her hand, she sets out in the direction of the well.

Her man never even casts a glance after her, he goes on slowly, very slowly, spooning the soup.

The well is a long way off. Beyond the wheat field lie some fifteen thousand acres of grazing land. On the edge of this lies the watering trough and the well for the cattle. The new beet field was part of the vast pasture until it got ploughed up, not long ago. That's why the well stands near the pasture's edge.

The woman goes straight on, stepping out briskly, her petticoats swinging. The young lord looks after her until she is nearly lost in the distance.

Then he says, with a start:

'My mount needs watering . . . Is there water in that well?'

The old foreman remains silent. After a while he speaks up.

'There is, your lordship. There's still water in that well.'

'Then I'll go and water my horse.'

He leaps into the saddle. The saddle is of yellow leather. The young lord's dandy riding breeches are of fine buckskin. Astride his mount he is a very handsome fellow, as he starts out at a trot in the direction of the well to water his horse.

The woman is drawing a bucketful of water as the Count rides up.

She looks scared as the young lord turns up at the well.

'Is there water in the well?' asks the young man.

'There is, Your Lordship, there is', answers the woman.

'Fine, then I'll water my horse.'

He slides down and leads his horse to the well.

The woman forgets to fill the bottle. Politely, she pours the bucketful into the trough. But the trough is large and dry, a bucketful doesn't go far. So she lets the bucket down again in the well and draws it again. Then she draws it a third time.

The horse dips its nose in the water, sucks in a mouthful, but it doesn't want to drink, it isn't thirsty.

The woman laughs:

'The horse ain't thirsty.'

'But I am', says the Count.

Without a word, the woman lets the bucket down again, keeps it dipped until it is filled, and pulls it up with circumspection. She fills the bottle, lets the top splash out over the well and presents it to the Count.

He keeps looking at her, his eyes gleaming like red coals.

'It's not water I'm thirsty for.'

'What else is Your Lordship thirsty for?'

'For a kiss.'

The woman looks him over with a flash of that confidence that only young and pretty women can show:

'That won't kill Your Lordship.'

'Nor do I want it to kill me.'

And he steps closer to her.

She flushes scarlet to the roots of her hair.

'My Lord, we're in the open fields here.'

'What if we are?'

'Just that.'

'Just what?'

'Your Lordship knows quite well.'

'No, I don't.'

'Yes you do . . . they'd see us.'

'May they drop blind, if they look.'

But the woman takes offence. She moves over to the other side of the well.

'Your Lordship mustn't come so near me. People do see, and they even see what you're after.'

The Count has a mind to follow her, but now he stops short.

'But look, this is the fifth day I'm out here for your sake. But you won't understand . . .'

'Indeed, I won't.'

'You're not getting away from here before I kiss you.'

The woman says earnestly:

'I've a husband.'

The Count keeps silent for a moment.

'What's the point of saying that?'

'That's for your Lordship to find out.'

'And I won't.'

His eyes burn like coals, showing to her what he wants, only too well.

'You love your husband?' asks the Count.

'I went with him before the priest', she says.

'I asked, do you love him?'

'It's not right to ask a wife that.'

'But that's what I want to know.'

'Then maybe Your Lordship should ask my husband.'

'Now listen. Don't you make a fool of me . . . I want you.'

'There's many a thing one wants that can never come to pass.'

'For you, perhaps, but not for me. What *I* want mostly comes to pass.'

'What must happen, will happen this time, too.'

'And what's that?'

'That your gracious Lordship get on Your Lordship's horse and leave me alone.'

'Look, I want no harm to you . . . I just wanted to have a talk with you.'

'There's nothing for you to talk about with the likes of me.'

'But there is . . . I didn't sleep all night for you.'

'Gentlefolk have enough pills to bring them sleep.'

'Only you could do that.'

'I'm not a witch.'

'I believe you are, for on Monday you looked me in the eyes and cast a spell on me. But now you slip away when I come near you.'

'Your Lordship has always Their Ladyships to console you.'

The Count says hoarsely:

'Now I'll kiss you.'

He makes ready to leap across the well.

The woman cries out in alarm:

'You budge, and I'll jump in the well.'

The young man stops dead. He smoothes his brow.

'You are a heartless hussy if you are having your fun with me.'

'How would I dare do that with an Honorable Lord?'

'Look at me. I'm worn out. I haven't slept these five nights. Have you no pity for me?'

'Oh, dear! Tell me truly my Lord, what you've eaten to-day.'

The Count is taken aback. For breakfast he had cold venison, a good helping. And two glasses of brandy, good and strong, for he wanted to warm himself for the day and gather courage to talk to her at last. He does not want to own up to this, so he says:

'For five days I've had neither food nor drink. I've just been pining for you.'

'It's like this, my Lord. My husband had nothing these five days but soup in the morning, soup at noon, and soup again at night. Isn't Your Lordship sorry for him in his poverty?'

'Why don't you cook him something else? Cold roast, jam on his bread. Stew for dinner . . . Fried chicken . . .'

'You shouldn't joke at the poor, my Lord. I can't even give the poor wretch a taste of gravy; there isn't enough fat in the house to do anything with the little flour we have. I cook for him with salt and water and I've not even potatoes to give him.'

'Now, then. That's where we should have started right away . . . If you listen to me I'll give you all you need. You can cook what you like.'

'Leave me alone, Your Lordship. I'm an honest woman.'

'And I'm an honest man. I'll stand by you, if you'll love me.'

The woman looks at him with hostility.

'My Lord, get on Your Lordship's horse and go away. That's the only decent thing you can do for me. As it is, we've been talking too long already . . . I don't know how I'll explain to my husband what we were talking about . . .'

'Think something up, then.'

'I could think of something, but I wonder whether you'd do it.'

'Anything you say.'

The woman closes her eyes and throws her head back.

'Something came to my mind . . . The men will soon finish hoeing . . . give them a good supper to mark the day, my Lord.'

'Why, gladly, but . . .'

'That's all I wanted to say.'

'And I'll get them a gypsy band, too . . . But you'll be there?'

'If every man's wife is there, then I'll be there, too.'

'But you'll dance with me?'

'If you dance with every woman, I'll have to.'

'But you'll kiss me!'

'If you kiss every woman, you may kiss me, too.'

'You're a witch, but never mind. I'll kiss every old hag, if I only get at you.'

'Then mount now, and go away.'

'Not I. I'll lead my horse and go along with you.'

'That'll never do, my Lord. You mustn't come with me. As it is, tongues will be wagging, because Your Lordship's been talking to me for so long.'

'What's your name?'

'Eve.'

'Then mine's Adam.'

'No. Your Lordship's called Victor.'

'There, you see: Victor means the winner. And I'll win out with you . . .'

'Good Heavens, Your Lordship must have a lot of time to spare to spend it talking to a poor woman like me.'

'Look here, little Eve, I wouldn't mind spending my whole life talking to you.'

'That would be a very long time for an Honorable Lord to spend.'

'The time that's long for me is till tomorrow night.'

'Then get on your horse and go at a gallop, maybe you'll get there quicker.'

The Count looks with coal-bright eyes into the eyes of the woman. Never before, he feels, has he come across such a nice woman. He is dizzy as he mounts. He waves once more to the young wife and gallops away.

She picks up the quart bottle and starts, deep in thought, on the way back to her husband.

4

'What the devil were you talking about with that young whelp of a Count?' asks Kis János furiously of his wife, as she returns with the quart of water.

'Something very good.'

The man stares at the ground. He has eaten up all the soup, and still he feels giddy with hunger. This has been their midday rest of one hour, he wants a nap, he is angry with his wife for wasting a half hour of his sleep, and instead of dozing off he must go on questioning her.

'Tell me, you bitch, or I'll finish you here and now.'

She sits down beside him on the grass. The men, seventy of them, are looking at her and wishing they knew what had gone on between her and the Count. But as to the women, and even the children, who had brought the seventy their midday meal, they stare and stare at her, and would give half their remaining days if they could gather what all that talk with the Count was about. On the plantation nothing goes unnoticed; however far away a woman is, they will always know when a man makes love to her.

'He said that . . . He asked if . . .'

'Don't you tell lies to me,' snaps her husband.

'He wanted me to tell him what the supper should be . . . he wants to give a free supper to all, when you are done with hoeing.'

The man's eyes open wide. He forgets all his anger.

'A supper?'

'That's what I said.'

The man harks back to his stomach . . . He is so thin, so wasted.

'And what's he giving for supper? . . . Thin soup?'

'Meat.'

'That's better. You've kept me long enough on soup.'

He wants to ask his wife why she, of all people, was asked about the supper. But his head feels dull; he does not care to say a word.

They glance towards the spot where the Count is in conference with the foreman. There is a throng around them. They see him mount and gallop away. The men nearby take off their hats and cheer, and throw their hats in the air, and cheer for all they are worth.

A lad, who runs past, shouts:

'If we finish hoeing by tomorrow night, His Lordship is going to give us a feast and we can all eat as much as we like.'

Kis János hangs his head.

'By tomorrow night?' he says; 'that means we must work all night.'

The woman is silent. She avoids her husband's eyes, and looks at the ground . . . She is thinking of the gypsies with their fiddles, playing for the dance. She shudders, and can almost hear the gypsy band . . . She feels the Count, as he draws near to take her by the waist and lead her to the dance.

Another lean man wriggles close to them.

41

'Have you heard?'

'I have.'

'He's a real gent.'

'Gent? He's a crook.'

'Why crook?'

'Wants us to work all night.'

'It's a full moon; it's all right.'

'All right for the moon . . . not for us.'

'One fat sheep to every ten men, for stew . . . A hundredweight of flour . . . And what's to go with it – forty pounds of fat, forty pounds of cottage cheese for cheese balls. And seven hundred quarts of wine . . .'

'Not enough', says Kis János.

'Not enough?'

'Not enough for me alone' says Kis János.

'Two pounds of meat for each man, if not twice that; two pounds of dumplings, if not twice that; good fat cheese balls, and seven quarts of wine for each man . . .'

'Not enough.'

'You can't put away six pounds of food and seven quarts of wine, that's near twenty pounds, in all.'

'All of that's not enough.'

'How much do you want, then?'

'The whole lot isn't enough.'

'The sheep are wethers, large old wethers . . . big, fattened beasts . . . You think you could put away all seven of them?'

'That I could!'

'And the dumplings from the hundredweight of flour, and the forty pounds of cheese?'

'I could.'

'And the fifty gallons of wine?'

'That, too.'

'What do you want, then?'

'All! All he's got. His forty-five thousand acres, and his castle, and his estate, his droves of cattle and herds of horses, his swine-herds . . .'

'And you'd put it all away?'

'I could. And himself for good measure.'

'You *have* got an appetite.'

'I've got one. Sure I have. I'm thirty-six years old and all my living days I've fed on foul slops. Even my mother gave me dish-water. When I go out to work, what do I take along in the field? A quart of water in my satchel, so I won't have to go to the well for a drink, but work on, instead of stopping for a drink of water . . . If I turn giddy at work, I take a mouthful to get over it . . . Waiting for the wife to bring me grub, boiled water is all it is . . . I swallow it . . . On that I go to work again . . . No, it isn't enough for me . . .'

'Not enough, maybe, not over a lifetime', says the other labourer; 'sure, no matter how much you eat, next day there you are just as hungry, feast or no feast.'

'Work there is aplenty, we won't run out of that', mumbles Kis János. 'All my living days I worked for this Count, Spring to Autumn.'

'Good thing', says the other, 'good thing there be this here domain, at least there's always work here.'

'From daybreak to nightfall I dig and cut the clod . . . might drop dead . . . and now to work all night for a supper . . . For what? . . . a bit of meat? . . . dumplings? . . . a glass of wine?'

'He's bringing the gypsies, too. A band.'

'And the gendarmes, isn't he? Rooster feathers, bayonets, and all?'

The other man, pondering, says haltingly:

'Aren't you in with us? You want to stay away? Don't you want to go to the supper tomorrow night?'

' 'course I want to. Just that it isn't enough.'

'What you want, then?'

'What I want? To eat this dog of a Count out of all he has, that's what I want.'

With hunched shoulders the wife listens to the talk of her man. She sits, overcome. She fears the morrow.

5

The gang of seventy work all night. They hardly heed the plants, just hoe and hoe.

After midnight the moon sets. It sets in the west, where the sun did before it. They are in the dark now and each lies down to sleep where he is.

The chill of the night draws in. They shiver. No one had thought of having to spend the night out-of-doors.

In the grey dawn the foreman comes to and gives a big shout. 'Up, fellows!'

The men stretch and get up. They shake themselves. In a long row they go to the watering well and wet their heads to shake off the sleep. They curse the lord who is sleeping snugly in a bed of down, while they are out, fretting in the field. And all for a supper. They swear and curse him, as custom will have it. But then they think of the supper, the fat mutton stew, the cheese balls, and laugh.

The young lads laugh and chatter like jaybirds before sunrise.

The old men are silent, like bears, now and then they hock and burp.

Somewhere on the Great Plain seventy men start on the day's work before the sun does.

The wives bring them breakfast. Whatever passable scraps they could hunt up in the house they bring along, knowing that the men have had a wretched night of it. For their part, they are tuning up for the evening feast. Their soles itch, they break into dance and laughter.

Kis János' wife also comes along and brings a good helping of food. Not broth, but proper cooked food. With plenty of noodles and plenty of potatoes.

'What's that?' asks Kis János.

'I went and borrowed', says the wife. 'I know you had a hard night, and there's a hard day to come . . . You must eat, or you won't last till night.'

Kis János looks into the crock. Then he says:

'What did the Count say yesterday?'

'What should he have said? He said nothing.'

'Nothing?'

'No. Nothing.'

'I had a dream . . . as if he had said something.'

The wife blushes.

'What did you dream? . . . What did he say?'

'You know that better than I.'

'I've forgotten it all.'

'Did he say such things that had better be forgotten?'

The wife hesitates.

'No, not such things.'

'What things, then?'

'Nothing at all . . . He asked, will a hundred pounds of flour do for the dumplings?'

'And then, what did you answer?'

'It won't do, I said, there being many of us, with all us women coming, too.'

'You said, the women will come, too?'

The wife pulls her kerchief forward over her eyes.

'What are you ferreting for? I talked nothing like that with the Count.'

'Like what?'

'What needs to be ferreted out like that . . . I said one sheep for every ten men, for they'll be with the families.'

'With the wives?'

'You have no children, you'll be all by yourself.'

The wife sighs.

Kis János pushes the crock aside.

'It was a shame to borrow', he says, 'what you borrow you'll have to give back.'

'We'll give it back all right.'

'What from? I can't make more than six pengös a week. Not after this, either.'

'You should eat it all the same. It's a long day, you won't have strength to stand it.'

'I will. I'll have strength enough for this day, Eve.'

The woman shivers slightly at the sound of her name. That is how the Count had said it yesterday: Eve . . .

'Eat now, eat', she persuades him, soothingly.

'I won't eat now; for what if I can't eat him out of his wealth tonight?'

'Of course not, how could you?'

'Even if I eat up everything, he'll still be a rich man tomorrow? You think he'll have something left to eat tomorrow, and the day after tomorrow? And after that?'

'I think nothing.'

'Well, then, go home, then. Take the food back, too. I won't eat today anyhow. You needn't come at noon. Just come at night for the dance.'

The wife cries out, aloud:

'What do you want from me?'

'And you don't come out at noon! . . . And out you come at night . . . or I'll go and fetch you.'

'You're sick, husband.'

Kis János smiles knowingly to himself.

'Well then, go home', he says, 'and don't let me say it again.'

The wife's eyes fill with tears:

'Oh, my husband, my husband! . . .'

She clasps her hands and begins to sob.

At this Kis János takes another tack. This is not at all the right way, he thinks. The woman is cunning, she will guess.

'Right, then', he says gently, 'I'll eat a bit.'

And he starts eating. Not much, but still, he eats. He even pats his wife's back, as one pats a good horse, and he no longer asks her to take away the crock. He watches her cover it with a kerchief and with grass, and bury it in the ground, so that the food will keep.

They have made headway by noon. They will finish the hoeing well on time. Already two men are let off from the gang to start building the fireplace.

At noon all the wives come out. Seventy women. As if by common consent, they are all wearing their Sunday best, even the old ones, to be ready for the dance.

Only the wife of Kis János is in her workday clothes. Kis János smiles at her and says:

'You are pretty enough as you are, eh?'

'If I am pretty for you, I am pretty enough any day', says the woman.

The womenfolk don't go home after midday, they stay on in the fields.

Early in the afternoon the hoeing is done. The seventy men leave the cultivated square mile behind. It is fine work. The huge field stands in fresh blackness up to the skyline, the young leaves of the plantlets flutter in the pleasant mild breeze.

The sheep have also arrived. The Count has sent not seven, but fourteen. The men do not cut up all of them for the cauldron, but share out among themselves what is left over.

Everyone is in high spirits. They make fun, they shout and sing. The open fields carry the voices far, and the wind weaves them into the distance.

Towards sunset the Count arrives, on horseback.

He is also dressed in festive attire. He wears a brand new suit of clothes, and patent leather riding boots. He looks as though he were taken out ready-made from a shop window. He wears a green hunter's hat and carries a rifle over his shoulder.

He is loudly cheered and shakes hands all round. With every man and with every woman. With Kis János, too, and with Kis János' wife.

'And how are you, Eve', he says to her and keeps her hand a little longer in his than he does the others.

Kis János says, laughing:

'Today we'll eat up Your Lordship's wealth.'

'Eat as much as thou art good for', says the young lord, who

46

thee's and thou's even the oldest men as if they were children, the way their lordships do.

He pats Kis János on the shoulder.

'. . . the workman is worthy of his supper', he says, as Jesus Christ said in the Bible. Except that Jesus Christ said 'worthy of his hire'. But the young lord does not care to put it that way, it might enter their heads to ask for a rise in wages. 'Supper', he thinks, is more fitting.

Kis János smiles.

'We've got an appetite . . . such an appetite, we'd eat up the country around, earth and all, like dew worms.'

'Better not, you know', says the young lord, 'what if you get indigestion?'

And he pinches the young woman's cheek, as if he looked to her for the protection of his lands.

Kis János laughs.

When the Count has left, he says to his wife:

'Still, you should have dressed properly. You've got a good dress, I bought you one.'

'I feel quite all right as I am', says the wife. She feels anxious.

They start to eat the supper.

Even soup has been prepared by the cooks. The soup is like so much oil. Fat and thick.

'Will you have some?' asks the wife.

'Is it good?'

'Very good.'

'I'll have it then. True, I ate a lot of soup in my day, but that was poor, thin dishwater, not good enough as feed for the sow . . . But I had so little good food, if you put it in a heap it wouldn't fill the crock you brought out at noon.'

The wife fills his dish to the brim, even spills it over, and he starts to eat. He is trembling with hunger, yet he has hardly eaten ten spoonfuls, when he feels full.

He is horror-struck and shaken by boundless rage . . . This is the day . . . and how will he keep his vow?

He gulps at the soup and washes it down with wine.

He feels his strength coming back.

The meat is handed round, a large dish of it. With a large piece of bread. He stares at it.

'Why don't you eat?' his wife asks.

'What's the hurry? I want to go on eating till daybreak . . . This was just the soup.'

The sun has set, and the moon, which was standing high, begins to show its polish.

The Count is there and everywhere. He talks to all, he throws his arms round everyone, and keeps coming back to them every few minutes, saying a kind word.

By this time the wine begins to work, the feast grows noisier and livelier. Kis János sees the Count going along, kissing the women-folk.

He wonders whether Eve will be next.

Eve also wonders, and trembles all over.

At this moment, out of nowhere a detachment of gendarmes appears.

Gay, good-looking fellows, they mean no harm; they just happened to be passing by. So they say. They have rooster feathers bunched in their hats. They shout loud greetings. Kis János laughs.

And he closes his fist round the knife with which he is eating.

Now the Count, making the round, kissing all, arrives in front of them.

He stops before Eve, bows . . . and does not kiss her.

Two of the gendarmes squat down on the ground near Kis János, when the Count asks Eve for a dance.

Eve looks at her husband.

'Go then, go', says Kis János. 'Dance. It's a good supper, dance it off, else it'll weigh hard on the stomach . . .'

The dance whirls wildly. Fifty or sixty pairs dance, the Count in front of the gypsy fiddlers.

Kis János begins eating.

He swallows a mouthful. He cannot hold it. He throws up and spits out.

'You see, Sir', he says to the gendarme, 'that's the trouble.'

'What's the trouble, friend?' asks the gendarme.

'Here's the good supper, and you can't get anything out of it, not even to have your fill once in a lifetime, 'cause you just can't eat.'

'Why can't you?'

Kis János looks for his knife on the ground and carefully wipes it clean.

'The poor man can't eat. Why can't he? 'cause he is poor. The poor man's food is sheer poison to him, isn't it? He gorges himself with the soup. When it comes to the meat, he is no good. The meat, that's for another to gobble up.'

'Eat now, eat', says the gendarme and looks keenly at Kis János.

But Kis János does not look at him. He looks elsewhere. He looks where the gypsy is playing.

'You haven't got two stomachs to put away all that. The poor man hasn't even a belly.'

In this moment the Count kisses Eve.

Kis János smiles. He turns pale, but he smiles. His hand freezes to the knife, and he thrusts it up to the hilt in the gendarme.

c.1930

People of the Puszta

TAKING BEARINGS

I was born and bred in the countryside and yet I knew as little of village life, as if I had been a city child. For part of my life all I knew of peasant ways rested on hearsay. I was born on the puszta and lived there until I was in my early teens.

Puszta, in the Magyar language does not mean only that boundless immensity of free, windswept steppe, resounding to the hooves of Petőfi's noble steeds, West of the Danube it means something quite different for the simple reason that there are no steppes in Transdanubia at all. Here puszta stands for a congeries of servants' quarters,[1] stables, barns and granaries, often the size of a village, built in the centre of a large landed estate. It cannot be called an outpost farm (or *tanya*) for it houses as many as a hundred or a couple of hundred families, instead of the one or two that inhabit an outpost farm. The Transdanubian puszta has a school and a church, or at least a chapel, usually snuggling a wing of the manor house. There is, then, also a manor house, in the middle of a large, lovely park with tennis courts, artificial pond, orchards, majestic avenues of ancient trees – the whole surrounded by a magnificent wrought-iron fence with a mudded-up moat nearby to remind you of past glory. Next in stateliness to the manor house, and now and then even surpassing it, is the oxen-stable. Next to that comes the house of the estate manager, nearly always hidden behind cedars and pine trees, by reason of some time-honoured custom. Less ornate than the manager's house is the bailiff's, and plainer than that, the chief mechanic's. These are usually detached buildings. The

---

[1] Servants on landed estates in Hungary were men hired for work with crops and herds by the year, against payment in kind, consisting of living quarters for their families, a small patch of land to grow their maize and potatoes, keeping of a pig and poultry, and fixed allowances of grain, lard and firewood. To this was added a token sum of money approximating one pound sterling a year. They lived and worked under conditions not unlike those of the Mexican *hacienda* peons. – Tr.

servants' quarters on the estate are anything but stately. The estate servants live under a single roof, in long, one-floored houses, which are much like the slum-barracks on the city's outskirts. Their living quarters are separated by thin walls. Every long low house is a series of habitations in which one common kitchen with an open range separates every pair of rooms. According to a law passed at the beginning of the century, there must be only one family to one room. In many places this law is already being observed. But there are not a few where it is not. In Somogy county I have seen many an estate servants' house which did not even have chimneys. The smoke escaped by the doors of the shared kitchens and each of the rooms housed several families. It gives you some idea what this means if you remember that the estate servants tend to be prolific, with six or seven children – and often enough even nowadays ten or twelve in one family. A few paces from these dwellings which stretch at random among the stables and barns, are the servants' pig-sties and hen coops, where they can keep an eye on their few domestic animals: the right to tend them is part of a servant's yearly payment in kind. By the findings of our ethnographers these sties and coops are still being erected along the lines of the architectural models that were valid in the Central Asian homeland, built of clay, wattle and a few props. On most pusztas there are three or four of the long low servants' houses: a separate one for the cattle drivers and a separate one for the coachmen, who in the tradition of the puszta's social hierarchy are superior to the cattle drivers, although neither their living standards, nor their work conditions are better. Lowest in esteem are, not the swineherds (as one might think, judging by the village), but those who work in the tobacco fields.

Nearly one half of Hungary's arable land is cultivated by the servants of the pusztas. In morals, customs, outlook on life – in the very way they walk or move their arms – this social stratum differs sharply from any other. Hidden, tucked away, beyond the villages even, they live in complete isolation. Due to their day-long labours, not excluding Sundays, they hardly ever leave the puszta. To seek them out in their habitat, I submit, is a more difficult undertaking than to study a Central African tribe – on account of the long distances, the bad roads, the peculiar Hungarian conditions, and also their primordial distrust of outsiders. Literature has not treated of them either, at least not up to the years after the First World War. They live in a community, curiously musty, yet invigorating both to the body and the spirit. In many ways this community reminds you more of the ways workers in a factory belong together, than of the way villagers do. Still, even that doesn't convey it. The puszta is a world apart. Its inhabitants' usage and vocabulary are unique: so are their dreams and fantasies, in the nature of things.

I still recall the stark wonderment, the throbbing in my throat the first time I was taken to a village, at the age of eight or nine. For weeks on end it held me captive, enthralled. The fact that there were streets, houses arrayed evenly side by side with streets between, filled me with unceasing amazement; with markets, too, the purpose of which I could in no ways conceive. It took threats and coaxings to make me set foot there even weeks after, so overwhelming was the din of the heavy traffic, the coming and going of men, carts and oxen, cows and children in that confined narrow space. Up to that time I had not seen any two houses arranged with a definite intention, made to stand in line alongside each other. Now, insatiable, I pondered the endless number of houses, that oppressive order and congestion. The secretive, disciplined regularity of a jail's corridors might impress the soul as those streets impressed mine, with their fences, gateways and the houses squatting inside . . .

Back at home, as I said before, only the manor house was fenced in. I should have added, had I not taken it for granted, that the people of the puszta were enjoined to pass along that fence without loud word or song, and, by some custom of ancient but obscure origin, without the enjoyment of tobacco. These injunctions, not unnaturally, were kept in observance by constant disciplinary action and frequent chastisement of the youthful element. To my childish heart there was yet another accessory to the idea of a fence – dogs. Dogs the estate servants were not allowed to keep, unless by virtue of a special permit given for some special reason. Their dogs might have done harm to manorial property, although what kind of harm is difficult to imagine, since the deer by that time were keeping well away from the puszta. Or alternatively they might have incited a degrading passion in the numerous manorial pedigree dogs. At the sight of the village houses strictly fenced in and guarded as well by snarling hounds, clearly I conceived the notion that they must all be inhabited by noble Counts, stand-offish genteel folk, not to be trifled with – in which, after all, I was not so far wrong.

Whether by bashfulness or some other vague sense of shame, for a long time I did not come to regard the people of the puszta as belonging to the Magyar nation at all. As a boy I could not reconcile those people I knew with that valiant, warlike, glorious people, the Magyars we were taught to be in that one-room school at the puszta. The Magyar nation lived in my imaginings as a blissful, distant people: I should have loved to live among them. In my dismal surroundings I languished for these heroes of my dreams. Every nation, I am sure, shapes a resplendent image of itself. I took this image for reality, I was after it in hot pursuit, while in effect I was denying ever more often the living exemplars. Much later, abroad in France, in Germany, realization came to me. It was painful and humiliating, my lofty internationalist principles notwithstanding.

. . . The people of the puszta, as I know well from experience that involves my own being, are a servile brood. The people of the puszta are submissive, and that not for ulterior motives or out of good sense. You can tell by their glance – a bird has only to cry and their heads jerk up – that it is with them almost a matter of the blood, an inheritance implanted by the passing centuries . . . True, they must be egged on to the work in hand. But why should I assume that this is incompatible with their passion for obedience? What social stratum, after all, is not kneaded together out of opposed ingredients? Clearly, these people cannot be understood at a glance; they must be closely examined from every angle. The truly servile are servile about what really matters. The arm may move slowly, but the soul is nimble in bending.

My instinct tells me, and that with the force of an ultimate conviction, that, even in those bygone centuries of *cuius regio eius religio*, no coercion was needed to make them fall in there and then with their overlords' frequently changing insights into the relative virtues of the one or the other of the Christian religions in matters of salvation and general usefulness. I am convinced that as soon as news reached them of their overlords' conversion or reconversion, they instantly concurred with his views and out of their own free will, with the bailiff in front, marched in procession from the Roman to the Helvetic church, or back from the Helvetic to the Roman, with song and frolic. Although it is shameful to confess, and pains me, I dare not take pride in and assurance from the faith to which I was born, since I know why it came to stay with the hereditary baronial family in the seventeenth century, after they had shifted their creed a number of times. I was a small boy when the puszta changed hands and passed from this same family to the Budapest firm of Strasser and König. Had the principle of *eius religio* but survived for another three centuries – a mere trifle in the eyes of eternity – my features, which now strike my friends as mongoloid, would doubtless bear semitic traits in my own discerning eyes. To say nothing of my soul proper, the psyche.

Two rising families

If the people of the puszta let the world glimpse just one smallest particle of that astonishing order of things in which they exist, they would have to renounce it root and branch and turn against themselves. That is how utterly the pattern of their lives contrasts with the order of things that reigns above them. Their own world, the nether stratum, is a warm mud-bath. Icy foreign winds drive over it. He who leaves it loses touch within a year or two, while his psyche and nervous system race through the stages of human development from primeval man to, say, the condition of a caretaker in a lodging house. But he who stays on, withdraws shivering at every touch of the world above: a fierce world, frozen like the hard crust of the earth, an empty shell of formal ethics and principles, which, let us admit, contains but the barest spark of life. A perilous world, with its laws, customs, private property, sex-life – who can pick his way among them? To that, too, you must be born.

* * *

Considering how families down the centuries have accumulated riches or made fortunes in our own machine-age, the ethics of my family's acquisition of worldly goods can come under censure only on the grounds that lesser results are less easily justified. My father's father was a shepherd. A head shepherd. Anyone with only a nodding acquaintance with that occupation in the closing decades of the last century will smile beforehand. He was, then, head shepherd to the Prince Eszterházy. And later on, to the lessees.

As to the precise nature of the arrangements under which that office was operated, he was the last person from whom they could be gathered, even by myself, and, I must assume, also by the incumbent Prince. When asked, he would embark on involved elucidations, and talk for hours on end about breeding, strains, first-fruit, seventh, wool scouring, tegs, tail-docking and allowance for staggers. The upshot was at times that he called nothing his own, he was 'a beggar and a servant', at other times, that to all intents and purposes the sheep were his, and he only handed over a couple or so to the manorial kitchen when he felt like it. The fact of the matter was, that besides his yearly payment in kind he had some direct income in proportion as the flocks increased. The first flock which he tended for the Prince, when he was a young man, had considerably grown with the passing years. There were times when he had as many as five or six shepherd boys working for him. There were years when he had no less than five thousand sheep. He was a power, not unlike the nomad rulers at the time of the migrations. Indeed, how many sheep did Árpád have? Be it said in my grandfather's honour, that he knew not the arrogance of possessions; rather, in his straight back, his arched chest he disported that chieftain's pride, the arrogance of freedom. That was the good life! Of the wool he received a certain share. The yeanlings he had to report. But to verify the loss of a sheep he had to deliver only the skull: later on the hide, too. In latter years the *seigneurs* became aware that sheep are milked, and that their milk makes tasty cheese, which had once been thought fit to be munched by peasants only. The world was going to the dogs.

But by that time grandfather had a vineyard in the next village, a house and plot in the district town, a son in the county administration, a son keeping his own inn, a daughter also installed in her own inn, a daughter married to a master cooper, another to the owner of a threshing machine, and another son – there's no saying what he did not have. He even had an altar with his name in gilt letters on it donated to the church of a nearby village. All this was due to grandmother, for on his own part he was a man of contemplation and peaceful ways, humming tunes, carving ornaments and generally taking it easy: as long as he kept a burro, he would settle sideways on the back of the well-fed donkey, leaning with his right hand on the animal's head, as in a rocking-chair. It was the way he journeyed, all through his life.

. . . Our grandmother was a tall, dark woman with a commanding glance, taller by a hand's breadth even than grandfather. She came from somewhere in the upper county, also from a puszta of course, and also Prince Eszterházy's. The grenadier stature and strong will was her gift to the family. She also was of shepherd stock, but of what provenance otherwise, I never found out. The only one of her kin she ever let fall a word on was a grandfather, a certain Börcsök László, who was 'an uncommonly tall and handsome man', and much travelled; each year he took the load of silver *thalers* to Vienna for His Highness, all by himself. Of all those of my forebears whom I had never seen, this Börcsök lives foremost in my imagination. I see his slender body, his lively dark face, I hear his fiery speech. I can see how he plops from the saddle in front of a hostelry, fingering his guns, how he enters the tavern. My elder brother was the dead spit of him, grandmother used to say. Stabbed to death he was at the age of twenty-nine, on the third day of October in an uncertain year of the eighteenth century, that day, like other days of commemoration our grandmother spent with prayers and fasting, mourning his memory, for she was religious beyond imagination. We, the children, had to take part in her devotions and loud supplications for the late Börcsök's salvation, who had passed without the Sacrament. To Purgatory, it was hoped. Such is the hold of tradition.

What kind of a woman was grandmother? How did she make out with grandfather? I was terrified of her. I remember best her icy feet – we and all our cousins had to clasp them, when she lay in her coffin, poor soul – so her ghost would not walk.

A good deal later, when our grandfather divided his days carefully between the singing of litanies and the guzzling of liquor, he turned to me after a long silence spent in front of the press-house, and haltingly, as if digging up at last an answer to some question of fifty years ago, he said: 'I had a girl recommended to me from Gyulaj, and one from Pula, and one had already sent along her kerchief. Her father was a shepherd on his own, that's what you want, János – people said. I didn't. A servant's son should keep off the in-laws' house, he's dirt under their feet, he should duck under at home. I could have found a better looking one, and better-off than this Náncsi, but she used to bring out the clean linen after me as far as a day's journey on foot, even before we were married. I haven't regretted it', – and with an upward jerk of his head he immersed his clouded glance in mine. My grandmother at that time had been dead ten years. Only then did I hear her Christian name for the first time. This childish name as if by magic made her come alive, a sinewy virgin, a contrary young wife, who later on was more of a disembodied principle within the family – the directing genius of tenacity, ruthless parsimony, unbounded ambition.

* * *

In an admixture of a different set of forces my maternal grandmother cut a figure of similar stature. And it was more than just chance that on both sides of my family a woman was in command, directing the strategy. In this sultry, primeval world that conserved so much of the tribes' body-heat, a woman ruled in each branching bush, a mother.

They did not rule by subduing the men; the men would roam the outer fields for weeks on end, they did not sleep in the houses even in wintertime; mostly they did not even have a sleeping place at home – in the dark hole where a family squatted in each corner. They slept in the manorial stable, to keep an eye on the beasts by night as well. To a degree it may have been also the worries that scared them away from home, the unending complainings, the crying and squealing, the birth of the children and their almost as frequent dying – such matters were for the women. And as for them, they took it on, with fierce determination, like so many she-animals; measured by their lot, the men were as free as the birds of heaven. Everything turned on the women: if a family was rising somewhat, that proved the woman's forcefulness, if going to seed, the woman's fecklessness.

My maternal grandmother was a genius.

I am using the word calmly, I have by now fully grasped its meaning. If my paternal grandmother wanted to lord it over the unruly future by erecting bastions out of florins, and would have sacrificed her own and her followers' welfare if not life and limb for sixpence, my mother's mother set her faith in the power of the human spirit. She was an educated person of astonishing factual knowledge; well read, not only by the standards of the puszta, but by those of the district even, indeed, of the whole county. She had been a servant-girl from her ninth year on, serving at the butcher's, the innkeeper's, the clerk's, the Jewish grocer's; finally, she served as first maid for four years at the house of a Director of the brewery at Kőbánya. Here she learnt that life can be different from the life her parents led. Here she met my grandfather, and with an ardour touching on idolatry, never exhausting itself in a lifetime, she there and then fell in love with his truly un-usually handsome features, his politeness, his distinguished name – he was called Louis – and, above all, I believe, with his un-paralleled helplessness. Grandfather had been discharged from military service at that time; he had not returned to his native village, but had taken on work in the factory where grand-mother was in service with one of the directors: for he was a wheelwright.

Whenever grandma mentioned her husband's occupation, even when she was very old, she stopped short for an instant, allowing her glance to make the round, severely. Let me, too, bow before the defiant vigour with which every member of the family, ex-cepting grandfather, adhered to this title. For grandpa was in effect a wheelwright, even if he only learned the craft when he was a man with a fully grown moustache. He came from County Békés, from the village of Gyulavári; when he was sixteen, in the Great Drought, he enlisted in the army for eight years' service as proxy to someone, for the sum of seventy florins, there being little use for him in the fields anyhow, and there being moreover eleven brothers and sisters at home. He was of such slight build, that after the recruiting his mother had to pin up the white mantle of the Uhlans for him, so he could walk in it. He was detailed to the cavalry, and he was dead scared of horses. I was greatly astonished to learn that they hardly knew horses where he came from: East of the Tisza, they ploughed with cows . . . He was sent to the Kisbér stud-farm, to live among fifteen hundred wild stallions. He fed them and curried them for three years, bustling about among them with a thumping heart, when it came about that a journeyman smith from County Tolna crossed his path and took pity on him. They consolidated a friendship, and what a friendship! Can I ever hope to possess the power of the word to give but an intimation of its quality? They remained together all their lives and when he was seventy-two and nearly blind, my grandfather one morning set out like one demented to cross the border into the Muraköz, then under Yugoslav occupation, to touch with his hands the wooden grave-post he had carved for him and see whether it was still in good repair. This journeyman smith, then, arranged for grandfather to quit the stables and be taken on in the repairs shop of the stud-farm, where he showed himself unexpectedly handy with the carpenter's adze, of which he never let go again. The young smith, who was in all things my grandfather's exact opposite, being a boisterous hothead, after their release from military service dragged him along to Budapest which was beginning to boom, and there along from factory to factory, for they would only take employment where both a smith and a wheelwright were wanted. He was looking after grandfather and minding him, until such time when he laid this office into my grandmother's hands, having put their union on firm foundations by his approval, the sum of ten florins, and the loan of a bed. With only this, for he himself got married then. This was only right, they did all things in step, even their children were born at the same time. The one difference was that he, the smith, married into his native puszta, and into a position, wedding the smith's daughter at Ráczegres. No more than two months after, however, my grandparents were also installed there. By the implacable ordinance of fate the former wheelwright was smitten dead by a thunderbolt, and thus removed.

In other words, my mother's family started life like this morning's first shoot, a minute green dot on the soil, which not even the expert's naked eye discerns, whether it is growing into a nettle or an oak? However, the seed was first rate. Grandfather, by destination a tumbleweed before the wind, now, securely staked and tended, struck deep roots in the friendly soil; he was brimming with the joy of life and with daring projects. At the side of the right woman his life reached fulfilment, gaining a rich significance. In the scuffle of 'free' competition he was bound to go under, but here, in the static, mellow mould of human society, in a world of servitude and poverty, his quietude, his soft-spoken word, his Calvinist inflexibility gained a new justification, became the roots of life. A swarm of bees alighted before the tree in front of the workshop; he caught the swarm in a sack, and although he had never kept bees, within three years he had a centrifugal extractor of his own construction, and a yield of ninety pounds of honey, sold by grandmother on the spot, down to the last drop. He was a man of few words and smiling eyes, who never allowed a loud tone to come from his lips, but at one time he refused to take over an important official letter on which his name, that happened to be identical with the name of one of the aristocratic clans, showed a mis-spelling. Or what was that? The wheelspoke in his hand that he had been carving he thrust with cold fury and full force, without making a sound, in the face of the gardener, who had embarked on the billowing sea of curses, which in the popular versions involve one's mother – in this case, his. For he never uttered a curse. To my mind this still is the most astonishing thing of all: that no curse, no obscene word was ever heard in their house, that is, in the room and in that corner of the shared kitchen which was theirs. All around him the puszta was wallowing and bubbling in obscenity, everything was called by its coarsest name, but the words recoiled at his threshold and on his windowpanes. We, the grandchildren, who grew up in the muggier atmosphere of the spoken language, and at the age of five were well up in all matters that are common knowledge on the functions of the body and the relation of the sexes, on entering the wheelwright's work-shop underwent a change, instinctively. As a dog, coming out of the river shakes off the water, so did we shake off our accustomed imaginings and their current expressions. For a long time I believed that grandfather did not even know those words. He spoke with an accent different from ours, the dialect of the Great Plains – perhaps those words did not occur there at all. One single curse I remember hearing from him: 'May the Fire have burnt him when he was a day old', he said with gentle eyes, but a set jaw, of one of his sons-in-law.

. . . If anyone purchased a book somewhere in a distant village grandma would have notice of it a couple of days after, and by the good offices of the itinerant egg vendors and rag and bone men, with whom she was anyway on excellent terms, she would contrive to borrow it. When a French governess arrived at the manor house, she struck a deal with her to give me lessons each night in exchange for who knows what stitchings or embroideries, although there was no question yet of my ever getting any education beyond the primary school. I made French conversation at the age of eight behind the oxen-stable.

Yet in those days grandma was past her prime. She had already hatched a brood. When did she find time to read? No one knows. She worked from dawn to nightfall, cultivating, besides the plot they held in lieu of wages, also other plots, in sharecropping, which she hoed and weeded with her four daughters even on Sundays. For she was an atheist – even that word was known to her. There was no church on the puszta, anyway. Unfortunately, she took the printed word for gospel truth. Once she read that thick brown soup was good for the children's blood. For four years we breakfasted on brown soup, nauseated, though milk was sufficient, if not plentiful. She also read that children should be kept occupied. We never had a minute to ourselves. Further, that draughts won't hurt you and that merit will receive its due reward. She believed all this firmly, and looked with irrespressible confidence to the future, for surely, then as now the gloomiest subjects were tied up with the dainty blue ribbon of hope. She was the one to draw the moral of the novel, and to learn a lesson from the fate suffered by the young nobleman who lost his fortune on horses . . .

Two opposing worlds

At the time when I was beginning to think and to observe the world around me, the silent war between the families had already begun. I took it for something that had existed from the beginning of time, something as natural as the fact that the twenty-four hours of the day fall into two parts: it was dark by night and light by day.

The two families could not see eye to eye: they were of different stuff. I took this for granted, never giving a thought for the reasons, much less for their elimination. Each family was a separate country, with customs of its own, inhabited by races alien to each other. I could draw their precise geographical boundaries. Thus, Simontornya and Igar, where my father had relatives, belonged to Nebánd puszta, and to the north and east of that lay the country of my mother's people. The sky above them, naturally, was also different. Over the one it was replete with martyrs and saints, angels peeped from behind the clouds, in the moon at night Cecilia played the violin; out of the sky over the other only rain fell, soberly, or sunshine on the fields. We children were in between.

The two opposing corners circulated their own views, gossips and plans. This did not hurt, as long as it all remained inside their particular circuits. But there were points of contact, shorting the grids. Sparks in ever greater numbers jumped the gaps, crackling and spluttering. Wherever else the opposing views came to a clash, it was invariably in our own small family circle that the fuses blew. The air was ever thick with the tension of approaching storms and with the reek of sulphurous discharges. We adjusted, willy-nilly.

As I said before, the trouble was about salvation, especially ours, the children's. All of us had been baptized into the Catholic Church. Much it amounted to. 'Say the Hail Mary', my father's mother told me in the family gathering, with a meaningful glance at her son. Indeed, I knew of no hailing at all. My mother blushed, and in her helplessness let a demure, apologetic smile wander round. She was unfamiliar with the Catholic prayers, and although her mother-in-law had given her a beautiful prayer book with a carved ivory cover, there were so many prayers in it that even when she picked a couple and made us learn them by heart, too, they never turned out the right ones. My father knew all these prayers, and even if he was no practising church-goer, he expected his children to be familiar with them. He held this to be a matter of propriety. His religious ideas, if he did think at all on these matters, may have rested on the view that 'there's no knowing', after all. But apart from whether he did or did not believe in God, he regarded himself in duty bound to give his children a religious education, as everyone did at that time. Mainly on utilitarian grounds. For if people feared nothing, they would steal and rob, and what, then, would become of the world? In those days this administrative view-point was going strong; the priests advanced it too, along with the theological proofs of the existence of God. The family council, meaning my grandmother at Nebánd, arranged for us children to spend shorter or longer periods of time there or at Ozora village, where my paternal relatives had begun to take root, as they rose socially, cutting loose from the puszta. There was also a proper elementary school, not like the one we had at the puszta. My mother to begin with was glad of this project, as of everything that was apt to broaden her children's outlook and education. But soon she had every reason to protest against it, in her own gentle way.

At Nebánd we were first put through the milder rites of exorcism. Then we were initiated to the faith. Not that of the Roman Church, as I myself believed at the time, but that of the puszta, which differs not a little. I showed myself highly receptive. An entrancing fairyland opened up to me. Back at home we were hardly ever told fairy-tales, since in my maternal grandmother's philosophy their main purpose was to scare the children. And whenever according to her other tenet, we were being usefully occupied, in shelling beans, say, or making rag mats, where you could talk, she made it a rule to tell us of the times when she was a servant girl, for our edification; later, as she grew older, she used to tell us how she came to meet grandfather. But at Nebánd even in the dim kitchen there resided the half-naked Christ within a bulky gilt frame, floating in the air above his own grave with nothing visible to support Him, and a mighty wound on His chest. He was flying to Heaven, to His Father, who was an immense eye, lodged in a coloured triangle. Thirstily I followed His flight into a world of intoxicating miracles. Having met with hallowed men and women, I soon became conversant with devils, dragons and witches. At night, ghosts sat before the door. At Ráczegres only frogs squatted in the cattle-well, but at Nebánd a waterman kept looking out of it, particularly if I had him in mind before starting out for the well. That God sees everything, and is everywhere I interpreted for a long time to mean: everywhere at Nebánd. Magic was abroad: wizards walked in the night, the cows predicted wars by giving gory milk, the livery-coachman hurled the hatchet skywards with ghastly swings of his arm, from the middle of the sheepyard, averting hail. Between the utterings of two curses the women would call on sweet Jesus, their faces changing in that instant, as of one who steps from a dark cellar into the midday glare.

. . . I prayed a great deal, and returned to Ráczegres, a St. George, girt for the fight. I would sacrifice myself. In my daydreams I set out to convert my mother's family, who, as the people at Nebánd had it, were irretrievably bound for Hell. Did they receive me with a superior smile? They did not receive me at all. My grandfather took my hand in his, casually. (To kiss was for women, to have one's hand kissed, for the gentry.) He looked down at me mildly. 'And what be that round your neck, son?' he asked with his ash-glimmer smile. There was no irony in this, nor astonishment, not even interest. Yet it cut my heart. I slunk away and quietly pulled out of the ribbon round my neck with the Virgin Mary's image hanging from it, suitably worn only by girls – but in my supererogation I had asked for the ribbon myself at Nebánd, as a shield against the flames of Gehenna.

I was pained and confused by the indifference with which they faced up to sure perdition. We were sitting at supper, I was in the grip of a terrible excitement. I wanted to shout aloud, desperately, as one shouts at people who walk on the edge of a precipice: 'Grandad, you'll end up in Hell!' But I kept my peace, tongue-tied, as sometimes in a dream. This, too, was as in a dream: the sight of my grandparents' ghostly courage . . . my Grandad calmly fingered a chunk of bacon between his thumb and fore-finger, on a Friday, cutting slices with his pocket-knife. Easing them under his moustache, he swallowed the shiny white pieces, each one of them mortal sin incarnate. I looked at this tempting of providence in anguish, expecting Grandfather to go up in flames of sulphur and brimstone, or at least for a piece of bacon to choke him, for a lesson, and a miracle. Of such I had often heard, even from priests. I was afraid for him, and anxious, for I loved him, I loved him more than the whole lot at Nebánd taken together. 'You'll soon outgrow it', he said when, after a theological disputation, I was driven to confessing, and declared, provocatively, that I was a Catholic. I told him of all the evil things heretics of his sort were accused of over there. To this he listened with interest, yet as far as my memory goes, without any direct retort. 'Peasants', he said, and deep down this instantly went home to me, even though those others were ten times better off than he was, and there were among them by that time craftsmen and even a county official.

But the other Reformers in my family were militant. The subtle theological arguments of yore had coarsened on their way down the centuries, as they had with the wandering preachers. The disputation on the immaculate conception lost itself in obscenity. The dissent had turned them even against Mary, they jeered at her: Mary belonged to the Catholics. I kept silent for a time, then, imperceptibly, I sided with them. Next time Nebánd once more was visited by a heathen – worse, a renegade.

What an amount of whispering, coaxing, threatening, of angry outbursts was needed to wash me white again, not to right the balance of my soul, but just to turn it again towards themselves. Like the hand on the scales I now inclined towards one or the other of the two pusztas, as I plied between them. I had become two-faced, and realized it only when it was past repair: I was hired out to both sides.

Selections from Chapters 1, 3 and 4 of Puszták Népe (People of the Puszta), *1936*

Orderly Resurrection

I

May is lovely everywhere, and lovelier still in the Bishop's grounds. Particularly, so early in the day, around sunrise. The dew laughs in sparkling drops as if Our Lady had thrown down a handful of precious pearls in the night. The flower-beds are choirs, chanting their colours in tune, and the lilac blossoms, smothering the length of the fence, are humming their whites and purples. High upon the roof of the Bishop's three-winged palace the returning swallows sit in the breezy light, singing with pink throats, each tiny body for all the world like a fledgling priest, singing his first Mass.

Nothing in human form comes crashing in here for a long while.

Then a short man in top-boots enters through the vaulted doorway. He has a ruddy face, moustachios, and a feather in his perky hat. He whistles and taps his cane on his riding boots.

This is the bailiff. He is called Dömötör, and is two in one: a Magyar when he curses, a Rumanian when he scolds.

With short, strutting steps he makes straight for the farmyard. He halts before the stables and raps out:

'Old Énekes!'

Waiting a second or two, he calls again:

'Énekes!'

An old man comes running out of the stable – slight, scraggy, a peasant in tattered clothes. His thin hair is long and white; white, too, are his brows and his shaggy moustache. He holds a book in one hand, which he is awkwardly trying to hide.

'At your service, Sir', he says.

'What's the book you've got there?' Dömötör nods at it.

The old man turns sideways, as if the book might be there.

'The one in your hand', Dömötör snaps.

'This? – *The Blessed Virgin's Flower-garden*', declares Old Énekes.

The bailiff points up at the lilac trees:

65

'And isn't *this* flower-garden good enough for you?'

'It is, indeed, but out of mine here I'm used to saying my prayers.'

'Well, I never . . .' Dömötör laughs. 'I should have thought there were enough people in this palace to say prayers.'

'There's never too many to do what is right', says the old man meekly.

'Is the manure carted out?'

'It is, for certain.'

'And have the horses been curried?'

'I was just making ready to do that.'

'What, with the book here?'

'Not with that, with the curry-brush, Sir.'

The bailiff takes his *Flower-garden* away, asking:

'Have you got more books like this?'

'What for?'

'Never mind what for. Bring out the lot, and quickly! No more of your praying away precious hours. *Eins-zwei!*'

Clouds drift over the old man's blue eyes, fear hems in his kindly face. What is he to do? To tell a lie is to go against his pure heart, yet his books are dearer to him than bread. He would love to curl up like a hedgehog, but there is nothing thorny in his make.

'Stop cackling there like a brooding hen', shouts Dömötör.

'What must I do then to do the right thing?'

'Get the rest of your books out here!'

Old Énekes is hedging:

'It's the one you were pleased to take away I mostly used for praying.'

'And the rest of your prayers? Where do they come from?'

'A little here, a little there.'

'I mean, from what books?'

'From invention and recollection, mostly.'

Two doves flutter to the ground near them. They coo and place their feet softly, their feathers rising and falling like an accordion.

'Have you any more books like this? Answer me!' Dömötör keeps on.

'I must state that I have not', the old man squeezes it out at last. As if on the run from his own self, he hurriedly points at the doves, saying: 'What pleasing creations of the Lord! Given to us as a parable of meekness and of love.'

'Given to laying eggs I'd like to see them!' says Dömötör, swishing his cane through the air.

With a flurry the doves rise, their wings beating like the fluttering note of an organ-pipe.

'Whoop! Fly off with them!' Dömötör says.

The old man's eyes follow the birds in their flight, blissfully. At last he gently replies:

'I did – in my soul.'

Dömötör puts him rudely in his place:

'Give me a rest from that damn soul of yours, Daddy Énekes! In my soul I'm also a Bishop. But is it me getting into the coach-and-four? Not a bit of it – it's still His Eminence.'

'Begging your pardon, Sir, but it's not the four-in-hand that does it.'

'What does it, then?'

'Salvation, and the good life hereafter.'

Dömötör laughs heartily:

'So that's the horse you put your money on!'

Old Énekes flicks up his hands, as though to keep away the Evil One.

'You'll only give comfort to the devil with words like these, Sir.'

'You're crazy!'

'Me, Sir?'

'You – you, who else?'

A smile twitches on the old man's lips, and his eyes glint in impish innocence.

'It's not the man who wants to have a good life here on earth that is clever, but the one who is out for a happy life in eternity . . .'

The bailiff, who got a laugh out of this, too, is looking for a suitable answer, but before he can say anything, a boy dashes out of the cow-shed, shouting happily:

'Daddy, Dad . . .' He chokes as he sees the bailiff standing near his father. Hunching his shoulders, he gives a little chuckle and tries to slink back into the cow-shed.

'Hi, you!' Dömötör calls him back.

The lad comes forward and stands in line beside his father. He is a growing boy, slight and lively. He does not take at all after his father. Nor are his eyes blue, but black, small and so alert that they never stop roaming. His forehead juts out, he is fast spoken and quick of wit.

'And you – were you also saying prayers?'

'Not me – and who was, anyway?'

'Your Dad.'

67

'He'd better, he works with the Bishop.'

'And who do you work with?'

'I work with the cows.'

Dömötör roars with laughter. The boy's smart.

'What a son you've got there, Daddy Énekes – what a little
. . . !'

The old man puts his arm round the clever lad.

'A good father need have no bad son', he says.

'Nor a rich man bad money', the boy chimes in.

This goes down well with the bailiff, too.

'Come on, let's have another', he eggs on the boy kindly.

His father also prompts him:

'Say something clever now, Péterke!'

'Not even Mass is said for nothing', Péterke announces.

'Alright, ask for something.'

The boy sizes up Dömötör, turning over in his mind what to
ask of him.

'Let's see now, what book is that?'

'You can have it!'

Péter takes the book and looks closely at the title words.

'That's ours!' he says and hides it behind his back. He looks
up at the bailiff archly and remarks: 'It's the ignorant that need
books in the first place, not learned men like yourself.'

'So I'm a learned man, am I?'

'Each is learned, selfsamely.'

'And what does *that* word mean, "selfsamely"?'

'It means that the ass knows how to bray, and the horse how to
run.'

'And me, what do I know?'

'How to make the ass bray, and the horse run.'

'And what do you know?'

'I know, that there are at least two legs to each ass.'

'And your dad, what does he know?'

'My dad, he knows that we are not three here, but four.'

The bailiff looks round but sees only the three of them.

'And who is the fourth?' he asks.

'God', replies Péter.

Dömötör is much surprised by the answer. He can't think of
anything to say right away. He sniggers and fidgets, ill at ease.
He ends up by whacking his riding-boots with his cane and throws
in gruffly:

'That'll do.'

He walks on, giving a vicious kick to the odd pebble or twig. He turns back suddenly.

'This yard here is a regular rubbish heap'. Words fall over each other, as he splutters: 'It really can't go on any longer, Old Énekes! I've put up with a hell of a lot. But what about the new manager who is due here today? He'll wipe the floor with you when he sees this filth – and how! This is no place for saying prayers and indulging in learnedness, here you've got to work. Understand?'

Péterke looks at his father reassuringly, but seeing that the old man remains silent, he takes it up himself with Dömötör.

'No need to lecture us.'

'What's this you say?' Dömötör barks, taking a step forward.

'Péterke is no more than a child', the old man says to excuse him.

But the boy steps up bravely to Dömötör and speaks:

'I say that there's no need to lecture us in such anger, since it is us that did the work in this yard till now, and no one else.'

'How dare you talk back like this?'

'I may as well, since it's me that does the sweeping', says Péterke, and without waiting for another word, makes off towards the cowshed.

Dömötör follows him with a bilious look, then he turns on the old man, growling like a dog:

'Get out, you too!'

Old Énekes answers not a word. He bends his old head and slouches off.

'Have everything spick and span by eleven o'clock!' Dömötör shouts after him. Then he, too, leaves the yard.

All is silent for a while.

A swallow flies away from the edge of the roof. One by one the others follow, circling fast and flying far.

The sun rolls up in the sky and bursts over the palace's back part, a mighty torrent, rushing in. It swamps the yard, turns pebbles and chaff into gold and polishes up the beads of dew.

Soon Péterke slinks out of the cow-shed with his broom, stops and takes a quick look around. The bailiff is nowhere to be seen. His face brightens. He claps the broom over his right shoulder and sets out for the stable. He stops in the doorway and sees that his father is painstakingly currying one of the greys.

'What a pity that poor horse can't talk', he says.

'Why?' asks the old man.

'If he could talk, he would ask you not to curry him, Dad.'

The old man gets on with the work in hand:

'Now be a good boy and do the sweeping', he says at last.

'It'll only stir up the dust.'

'Go along now! Did you not hear what the bailiff said?'

'If I were bailiff I would also say a lot of things.'

'If this is how you obey, there is no future for you on this farm.'

Thereupon Péter takes the broom from his shoulder and props it up before him, as a shepherd would his crook. Turning something over in his mind, he puts on a serious expression and speaks as if he were addressing an audience:

'It's not working out at all the way you say it is, Dad. For on this farm here, and elsewhere too, the way to get on is the way I do things, not the way you do them, Dad. This book here – who got it back? Wasn't it me?'

'That was clever', says the old man, 'Now go and sweep up, there's a good boy.'

Péterke has the answer ready:

'Catch me sweeping you, silly old yard!'

'You are in a mighty rebellion!'

'That I am. And so should you be, Dad, for the tongue will ever get more done than a pair of industrious hands. There's proof, and most of all you've proved it yourself, Dad. For you've grown old here in this farmyard, and where did it get you? Not very far, for you were ever silent and never idle.'

'Look not for justice here on earth', the old man remarks sadly.

'And why not?'

'There is none.'

'The heck there isn't!' Péter contradicts. Justice there is, for sure, and not one single justice only. There's a couple of them. For there is a rich-justice which the rich man buys himself with money, and there is a poor-justice, which the discerning man gets for himself by the use of his brains.'

The old man listens placidly to the speech of the outspoken lad. He thinks on God and on the life eternal, when each shall gain his reward according to merit. He has nothing to say, he curries one horse after another, meekly, as though preparing to go with them into the hereafter.

Péter in his turn tires of making speeches, and goes out into the yard. Humming a tune, whistling idly, he shuffles back and forth. Now he picks up a shaving, now flings a pebble beside the fence.

Just whiling away the hours.

At last the new manager of the estate makes his appearance. He is a tall, distinguished looking gentleman. He wears a fine blue suit, and carries gloves and a walking stick. Dömötör paces at his side, gesticulating and talking incessantly. They are nowhere near the stable when they stop short.

'Énekes!' cries Dömötör.

The old man steps out of the door.

'Péter!' cries Dömötör.

Péter also steps forward.

Like a couple of recuits, the two of them stand in line before the two gentlemen.

'This is the coachman, and that's his son', Dömötör introduces them.

The manager looks the two hired men up and down, and turns to the old one:

'What's your name?'

'Énekes Ferenc, at your honour's service.'

'And yours?' he asks the lad.

'Mine's Péter, witness the bailiff.'

'Why need he witness it?'

'So he should also have a part to play.'

The manager turns with a faint smile to Dömötör, who remarks: 'This brat has always something up his sleeve.'

The manager pats Péter on the cheek and dismisses him along with his father.

'The old man looks reliable to me', he says.

'Quite reliable', says Dömötör, 'but not much use. He's old and feeble-minded, poor soul . . .'

They do not view the horses, nor the cattle. They stand talking a few minutes longer, after which the estate manager takes his leave.

'Now then, Daddy Énekes, how do you like the new manager?' Dömötör asks.

'He seems a kindhearted, distinguished man', replies Old Énekes.

The bailiff guffaws:

'Just imagine: came out of jail six months ago. Then he, the Jew he is, comes here fawning on His Eminence. And what with him saying as how he's seen the light eternal, he switches to the Catholic Faith, and here he is, estate-manager to the bishopric. Now I ask you!'

'The Lord rejoiceth more of him than of the ninety-nine which went not astray', says Daddy Énekes.

Dömötör is furious:

'Like hell He does!' Then he adds, hurriedly: 'See you have the large coach ready by five o'clock. Understand?'

'Yes, Sir, at your service.'

Again the bailiff whacks the leg of his top-boot as he goes off.

Daddy Énekes gets ready. He greases the harness and shines up its brass buckles. He washes and polishes the coach. He hums sacred tunes to himself and is filled with bliss.

At five in the afternoon Dömötör and the estate-manager take their seats in the well-sprung coach. The old man drives the two greys cheerfully, heading for the episcopal estate. As they arrive and the passengers alight, the manager turns to him genially:

'Don't you ever spit, Daddy?'

'I'm not one for smoking a pipe, Sir.'

'But even so, after all, you're a coachman.'

'All my born days I drove the horses without spitting, Sir.'

'And you never curse, either?'

'That I would never do, your gracious honour.'

'What kind of a coachman are you, then?'

'Just an old coachman, please your honour.'

A week later a new coachman is put in charge of the greys.

He is young, strong and a ruffian.

He spits and curses.

He bawls at the old man and hustles him. When no one is looking, he kicks him in the pants.

Péter sees how matters stand and boils with rage.

'I'll thrash this dirty scoundrel, Dad', he says.

'Don't, son. God will set all things right.'

'I wonder.'

The old man falls sick. He is bedded down in a corner of the stable, on a rickety old contraption.

The new coachman cannot stand the sight of him even there. He flings the curry-brushes at him, and every now and then the shovel and the pitchfork.

One Friday he tips him head over heels into the corner, together with his bed. He spills him out like a lot of rubbish.

Peter gets out his jack-knife.

'I'll cut out his guts', he flares.

The old man lifts up both hands and implores him:

'Do not hurt him, dear son!'

He can scarcely get the words out:

'Beyond, there . . . justice . . . will be done.'

Next day he dies in silence.

Half a day and a night long he is left to lie in the stable.

Péterke and the horses keep vigil over him. The stable flies buzz around him, and the ordinary flies from outside and all kind of fancy and gaudy flies settle on his composed, serene face and lay their eggs on it.

Then he is buried.

2

He lies in the proper graveyard, where everyone is buried.

Somewhat to the back of it, near the mighty fence.

His coffin is knocked together out of thin pine boards. It is unpainted, with large cracks through which to watch for the resurrection.

His grave is shallow and the earth presses gently upon him.

Énekes Ferenc lies among great ecclesiastics and great nobles, among the rich and the blissfully poor.

He lies and waits.

The days go by in peace, without noise or fuss.

He waits for the break of the light eternal, and the coming of justice.

His colour deepens by degrees, and his patient longing wastes him away steadily, bit by bit.

Irretrievably, he slumps inwards.

He ferments, according to the laws of organic change.

The fly eggs on his face hatch and indulge in childish delights. Vermin frisk about, hurtle and buzz round his face as though it were a pleasant ground of rolling hills. They climb over his nose and ears and slide impishly down into the vale of his cheeks.

They are many and of many kinds, as in human society.

They come grey and spotted, checkered and striped. The finest is a dandy green fly of metallic sheen. He is snobbish and darts about to show off his magnificent colour. He is finicky, refusing food, contemptuous as it were of Énekes Ferenc – a mere peasant.

The rest fall to, the more greedily.

Through the cracks in the coffin the odour of their feast wafts abroad into the soil. And mainly upwards to the surface, where it intoxicates the stray flies. The fertile mother flies are drawn along in swarms. Drooping, they lay their young, who, spying out as entrance dew worms' tunnels and cracks between the clods close in for the attack on Énekes.

The red-bellied, black-striped beetles cut their way up from below, scratching and splitting up the clay, sappers of the graveyard.

The old man experiences a time of fierce onslaught.

A dance is on.

Graceful little moths make free with him, gambolling about.

Next, in the soggy ammonia stench, come the tissue-eaters – hardworking, determined insects.

Last of all, the nimble mites which turn the old man into a neat skeleton.

Silence takes over.

Time alone ticks, like an unfathomable and perfect clock which has the Sun for its main wheel and for its lesser wheels the stars.

Its seconds measure the centuries.

Its minutes are millennia.

Ten minutes make a million years.

Its hour is eternity.

It ticks, and its hand, like a comet's tail, moves on, from hour to hour.

It is close on midday.

The hour strikes, resounding across infinity.

The angels form ranks as on parade.

The stars dance like dew drops on the lilac bushes at dawn.

God steps into the middle of the world.

The Day of Judgment has come.

The Earth, like a child's ball, bounces over into another universe.

Gay, beauteous angels step up onto it and sound the trumpets.

The world is ringing with their blasts.

Light pours down, like a rainstorm.

The graves burst open and cry out in joy.

The trumpets blare away, like unquenchable laughter.

The dead awake and throng out, frolicking.

Péter's eyelids pop open. He sits up. Sensing some miracle, he quickly takes stock, glancing round. He discovers his old father lying at his side and he is filled with joy. He draws himself up from the hips and has another look. He sees the receding walls of the grave, and flowers, such as no eye has ever seen at its rim. He sees the soft fragrant light welling in from above, And he hears the trumpets' blast.

'This is it', he says. 'There's never been the like.'

Grabbing his father's collar-bone, he gives it a shake.

'Dad! Dad!'

The old man does not feel at all like moving.

Péter shakes him harder.

'Get up, Dad, they're blowing their trumpets for all they're worth.'

At long last the old man's eyes open, slowly. He sees the down-pour of light, and is worried for having slept in too long, and he a hired man. Hastily he makes the sign of the cross, as he used to do when he was alive.

'This time it's called for, Dad', says Péter.

'What is?'

'Crossing yourself.'

'Why that?'

' 'cause it'll stand us in good stead.'

The old man has no notion at all of what a great day he has woken to.

Péter greets it with a laugh and looks on in delight.

'It's a fine day, isn't it, Dad?'

Énekes looks right and left in wonderment.

'I have never seen it so fine', he admits.

'From now on it will be like this for ever', Péter points out.

'Where do you take that from?'

'That's what the trumpets say. Don't you hear?'

'I hear them all right', says the old man, but I thought it was the gentry going out with the hunt.'

'Now it's us going out hunting, not them.'

'How's that?'

' 'Cause this is not their day but our day.'

The old one is still drowsy, and has not managed yet to come back into being. Peter grabs him by both shoulders and gives him an almighty jolt.

'It's the resurrection, Dad!' he shouts.

Énekes gasps for breath and the hollows of his eyes fill with tears.

He weeps for joy, like a child.

'Now is no time for crying, but rejoicing', Peter instructs him.

The old man wipes his eyes with his skeleton hands, and presently he asks:

'Where is God?'

'Out in the yard, likely.'

'Then let us go straight before Him.'

'Yes, right there', says Péter, standing up. Then he thrusts his hand in the old man's armpit and helps him up.

'How do we get out of here?' Énekes wonders, looking up at the sheer walls of the grave.

'Quite simply', says Peter, and he pushes the old man up with ease. Then he jumps out himself, and they set off among the empty graves.

They go on their way, every now and then stopping.

They well over with wonder and bliss.

For the Earth is like the Garden of Eden.

'You know, I did kill that coachman', says Péter.

The old man looks at him, taken aback:

'Not in truth?'

'I did, though.'

'And what happened?'

'I was in a dungeon twenty years.'

'Then you have endured the penalty.'

'That I have. But with Judgment at hand, it is as well to let sleeping dogs lie.'

As they cross the cemetery, a lunatic is rushing backwards and forwards, peeping into every grave.

'And who are you looking for, mate?' asks Péter.

'I'm looking for my wife', says the lunatic.

'And where would she have got to?'

'What with all this mess and insurrection, she's beat it.'

Straggling resurgents make their way along. Some are on their own, others are trailing large families: whole lineages show up.

Two apprentices hurry on, as if they were late for clocking in.

'Everyone is pushing – even here', remarks Péter.

'They are pushing in the right direction, at least', says the old man.

At the approaches to the gates there is a great throng. From afar the crowd heaves and whirls. As they come nearer it roars and crashes like the sea. Sworded angels are busy on both flanks and to the rear, maintaining order. An angel of rank shouts his commands in shrill tones above the turmoil:

'Atten-shun! Fall in! Orderly resurrec-shun!' The higher angels stand in a group apart, bearing themselves like a general staff.

Énekes and his son arrive and mingle with the crowd.

The commandant cannot control the flood. He draws his sword. Flashes it in front of them and shouts again:

'Fall in! Fall in by rank and title!'

It is a bewildering, strange gathering – bustling and gay, yet alarming. The clicking jaws rap out sounds, and grin when they are at rest. Eye-sockets stare greedily into the resplendent world. The light plays on the skulls in a great variety of colours. Feet patter, and arms flailing the air whistle like the reed-pipe, shriek like the clarinet or laugh like the recorder.

In the headlong rush the bones jangle in all manner of keys.

There are some jolly fellows playing the zither with their finger-bones on each other's shoulder-blades.

But nothing seems odd to them.

They know each other.

They see, and hear.

All things to them come naturally.

Above all, they push on and try to jump the queue.

'But why are they elbowing?' Énekes asks a man nearby.

'Because', says the man, 'each wants to get richer than the other.'

'How do you mean, richer?'

'Don't you know even that much?'

'I don't know anything. I only just arrived with my son.'

'Now listen, you sucking babe', explains the man: 'Each tries as hard as he can to be out of that door before the other fellow, so he can stake more claims.'

'Claims for what?'

'Well, land, or high timber, a brook for panning gold, or a mining site. Whatever he fancies.'

They are forced apart and borne forward.

The angel-in-command bawls at the top of his voice right beside them:

'Fall in! Fall in by rank and title!'

The old man and Péter exchange a glance.

'Funny sort of resurrection!' says Péter.

'It is a little queer . . .' the old man admits, then adds, confidently: 'But it cannot be that merit should count for nothing here.'

They fall back slightly to gain a better view and to look for an opening ahead.

'Step into line!' an angel calls on them.

'We're not in the army here!' says Péter.

An argument starts.

'Upon earth I lived in the service of God', protests the old man, 'Now is the time to be given my reward.'

'Your name?' asks the angel.

'Énekes Ferenc.'

'Your former occupation?'

'I was coachman to His Eminence the Bishop.'

'Then better get down to the end of the line.'

'Wherefore?'

'Because that is the place where you belong. First out are the Bishops, the Canons and the lords temporal. What is the idea? When all is said and done, you are a coachman. You cannot have this new world turned upside down right on the first day.'

The old man is aghast.

'I find it strange', he says.

'Strange or not, get down to the end of the line.'

'Pardon me asking, please, in whose name do you speak?'

'I speak for the organizers.'

'And would God know about this?'

The angel answers, truly shocked:

'Naturally! Everything is done in His name.'

'I find it hard to believe', Énekes shakes his skull.

'If you don't believe it, you shall see for yourself', says the angel and goes away to fetch the Commandant.

'My hunch!' says Péter and makes a sign to the old man to follow him.

They slip away into the crowd and push as hard as they can.

But the Commandant catches up with them; he grips each by the shoulder, the old man with his right, Péter with his left.

'Do we proceed in order, or do we not?' he turns on them in anger.

Énekes confronts him:

'We do – in order of merit.'

'Then move on to the rear!' The angel hustles them out of the throng and points down the line.

'Be off!'

Feverheat races through the old man's bones and flames leap from his ribs. His jaws tremble, his neckbones screech. This last injustice gives him miraculous strength. He straightens his back.

He stands like a blazing pine tree.

'I'm not going!' he says, threateningly.

The angel makes ready to draw his sword, but Énekes jumps clear.

'You were right, Péter!' he cries, and with a lightning jerk unhinges his shank-bone and swishing it overhead like a flail, cuts down the rows right and left.

'Let 'em have it, Péter!' His shouts rend the air.

Péter is already laying about with his shankbone, thrashing them for all he is worth.

Swaying on one foot, they mow down the crowd. It's a howling rout.

The angels sound the bugles to call in God.

God appears; a dead silence sets in. He makes a sign to Énekes and Péter to click their shankbones back in and come before Him.

Énekes and Péter obediently do as He says.

'Why are you disturbing the peace?' asks the Lord.

'Because the angel wanted me to stand to the rear', the old man replies.

'And why did you not want to stand there?'

'Because I suffered and endured all through my earthly life in order to gain happiness now.'

'And is there no happiness for you in the rear?'

'None.'

'Why not?'

'Because ahead of me I see those who were thieves and evildoers during their lifetime.'

God looks with compassion upon Énekes, and asks him:

'How did I create you?'

'You created me good, and poor.'

'Then be good and poor, taking your place in the rear.'

Énekes looks at his son, wondering what to do.

'All the same – don't let's go', whispers Péter.

They stand; and do not move.

Sadly, the Lord looks long at them.

'I regret that I resurrected you', He says at last, in disappointment.

'That can be put right', replies the old man, hurt by this time. He calls his son: 'Come on, Péter!'

Together they set off, back to the cemetery. They return to the grave from which they had risen a while ago, stop at its rim, look down into it. Then both turn round, and wonderfully impelled, as if by a single thought and the same deep undying bitterness, they cry out in one breath:

'And no more trumpetings for us!'

Whereupon they quietly lie down again side by side, scrape back the clods for a cover, and fall asleep for time and eternity.

1931

79

PINIONS OF POVERTY

Pinions of Poverty

The winter dawn stirred.

Lighter than lightly it moved in on the cambric white of the land, as the silver haze that changes its colour when the day brightens. The mirror of the human eye could barely capture it, but the birds saw that the sun was on the move.

The stars, blinking lazily with heavy eyelids, dozed off in the eastern sky. Soon the pale light set out, as a breath of joy. On its way, as it neared the village, it ladled the white trees out of the night's dimness, then it seemed to stay on for a wink or two in the garden of old Ehedi Ambrus. Two apple-trees spread their branches in the back of the yard, not far from the shingled cottage. One was an old tree, disporting its years and the profusion of its branches in the sky. Next to it stood a small, sprightly tree, evidently having the old one for its grandsire. Here the fledgling light lingered, whirled round in silver swirls between the branches of the two trees, on which the snow squatted in thick streaks like the fat bacon that comes to the poor man in the fairy tale. The light gathered there, coming to a rest between the snowy branches. It swayed and fluttered, as if trying out its wings.

What a beautiful delusion – you might think.

Yet it was true – between the two apple-trees the light was stretching its wings; and after a few flappings it took flight, blowing the crystal snow into the air. And high in the dawn above the two trees the snow danced around in great whirls. From the thickening air the wafting light picked out two shapes, twirling them gracefully, bobbing and swinging them, as though they were two maidens at the dance, and led them towards the roof of the shingled cottage. So do the fairies fly.

Gently they mingled with the warm smoke which reluctantly seeped through the roof's weathered shingles into the outer cold. And as the two snowflake apparitions came near the smoky roof, their wings melted away and soon the dawn's own children were gone.

Only the smoke kept on seeping through the cracked shingles. It did not just seep, it rolled and coiled upwards and puffed small buxom clouds at the drowsy stars.

Perhaps the house is on fire – you might think.

But the mindful neighbours said nothing. They looked impassively at the dense rolling smoke, knowing well that in these parts the old shingled cottages have no chimneys to them. The poor old smoke must find its way out into the world as best it can, once it had done with brooding among the rafters, with no bacon-ribs nor sausages hanging there to cure at its pleasure.

Such a poor man was old Ehedi Ambrus, who lived there underneath all the smoke. He had not slept all night, although the nights are long enough in early winter, when quaint twigs and flowers freeze onto the window-panes and the endless dreams of a hard life well up in the silence. He tossed this way and he tossed that way to make the night go by but as it got past the midnight hour, he began instead to watch the window, wondering whether the dawn was astir yet.

When a very long time had gone by, and the faintest of tints touched the window, he silently got up. He moved slowly and trod softly in the dark room so that he would not awaken his son's wife as she lay by herself in the other bed, breathing quietly; and so that Györke, the only grandson, should not waken on the bench.

There was hardly a rustle as he got into his clothes.

But Györke was only dozing that night and at the old man's shuffling he came wide awake but made no move, in order to keep his open eyes a secret. He was looking on to see what his grandfather was up to so early before dawn.

For somehow this dawn was unlike any other.

Old Ehedi slowly made his way to the iron stove, noiselessly took off the rings from its top and filled the stove's belly with a good deal of wood through the large round opening in the top. Then he put back the iron rings, carefully fingering their places. Then he put a handful of dry twigs into the stove's mouth and lit them pushing a small twist of straw underneath. The dry faggots crackled and burned merrily, but soon the green wood behind the flames began to sizzle and to splutter in the fire.

'Mind you catch fire', said the old man under his breath.

Once more he stuffed faggots into the stove's mouth in profusion, the flames roared up, and red shadows flickered across the tiny room. But the green wood kept weeping and frothing in its misery.

'I'll toss you to the devils', muttered the old man.

84

Like a peeping moon, Györke was grinning on the bench. His heart was open to his grandfather, like a table laid with food. But he was full of mischief and his fluttering mind took delight in listening in to the endearments the old boy had for the green wood. There was more morning fun as he stuffed some of the plank from the bed into the stove's mouth. Of course, it wasn't really a good plank. It came crashing down every time you tossed and turned in the bed. But the plank that was such a bad servant at sleeping time, now stood its ground for it kept creeping on after the green wood until it had stealthily taken the flame wholly into the body of each log.

Now they burned good and fast.

Up on the roof the smoke thinned out.

The day was breaking.

'All your snivelling didn't help you, did it now?' said the old man in a mood of victory.

Then he looked round in the dim room. Its frosty windows glinted as silver glints in its gayest mood; they softened the morning light so that inside the room you looked like a swaying shadow. So did old Ehedi look as he haltingly stepped hither and thither probing the silence and the solitude he desired. First he peered out of the window, but the outside world wasn't showing, so he began scratching away the frost under the twigs of a tiny ice-shrub and he looked with one eye through the little hole into the outer expanse as if he were peering down a rifle barrel. Then he glanced at Györke, bending down gently over him: and seeing how sweetly the lad's eyes were drenched in sleep, he then looked at his son's wife who was still breathing quietly, like the hidden springs of summer. And so, having made sure that only the cat was blinking under the stove, and everybody else was rocking gently on the waters of sleep, he stealthily pulled out the table drawer and took out the green army post card which his son Gáspár had written from the battlefield and which had come to hand the day before. He turned the card and held it up in the milky dimness, but the letters swam like tiny fish and the light was too faint for his old eyes to hook them in. Then he turned to the humming stove, holding the card with great care, as he would a rare bird that had alighted on his hand.

There he settled down near the stove door and opened it, so that the light of the fire might flood out from behind the red cinders. He held the card into the warm frame and though last night they had read the writing on it repeatedly – silently each for himself and aloud together – he once more settled down to it and read out the message, halting time and again. His heart lay like a mere whiff of warm, new-baked bread on his faintly moving lips; but the letters, once they had one by one risen from the green field of the card had a vigour all their own. They rose in the air, audibly, like birds.

Perhaps they would just alight upon a silver shrub on the wintry window.

Györke listened . . .

My dear Father – the writing went – My beloved wife Vilma, My darling son Györke. These few lines are to tell you that I am in the Wooded Carpathians. And the day before yesterday it looked to me that I wouldn't ever write you any more. But then I somehow got the better of the enemy, that is, of my share of them . . .

Here the old man allowed himself a longer break, and nodding his head he added his own bit:

'That's the way, son.'

Then he went on reading at the firelight:

Further I am to tell you that due to the above I am now a lance-corporal. Likewise, First Lieutenant Bacsek said, though he laughed at it, that they're going to pin on my breast such a medal, the king himself, even Francis Joseph will slap his right knee for pleasure . . .

The old man put in with conviction:

'So he should.'

To wind up, he read from the card:

Here the winter is so severe that the birds die off. True, they are also being shot.

Which concluded the message. Old Ehedi held the green card in his hands a while longer. In the heat of the fire it had curled up like a rare flower, closing after it had given off its scent.

He held the card, looking far away from the fireside, looking through the milky light which was now gathered in the bare little room and was shedding its mellow warmth upon the sleepers.

Then he got up and put the card back in the table drawer, meticulously, as old people do. Again he went to the window where the warmth made drops of water gather and run down the melting ice-twigs like so many pearling dew drops.

'Györke boy', said the old man softly.

Györke pretended to come awake at his grandad's calling, yet still briskly enough to earn praise. He did not fail to get his reward, for the old man said:

'Because you were so quick I'm taking you with me to the woods.'

'Shall we just be walking?'

'Not just walking, we'll take the shank's pony sledge.'

Györke jumped off the bench and in a couple of winks he was ready to start out with the sledge. His eyes sparkled, he kept laughing for joy, for to go to the woods with the shank's pony sledge in a tremendous, sparkling snow was a great thing.

What with all the rejoicing, his mother also woke up and, smiling bashfully for having overslept so badly, she quickly milked the goat and boiled up the milk on the roaring fire to let them have hot milk before they went to the woods.

They drank and set out.

The sun was just creeping over the edge of the silk-white world. It let its silver pallor trickle into the unbounded whiteness and mingled a touch of red with the silvery light. The trees stood out like heaven's lacework and the fields shone like some benevolent giant's mirror.

'Oh, how lovely!' said Györke.

'There, you see', said the old man beaming, as if he were sole possessor of all that the eye drinks up in delight.

Upon the vast snows the sledge hardly needed pulling, it slid as if of its own will. It was quite a large contraption, with the axle-bars between the runners and four lades to keep the load in place; and two ropes in front to sling over one's shoulder and pull the load over any rough patch.

A poor man's winter wagon, then.

In other words, a shank's pony sledge.

Györke loved it, for it ran on downwards even on a slight slope like a large playful dog and kept slyly loafing behind on the ascent as if it were admiring the hoar-frost blossoms on the trees or in silence watching for birds that flicked shadows across the snows or, touching down, whirled silver dust onto the trees.

'Who made the sledge, grandad?'

'Your father, when he was a lad', said the old man.

The boy sighed and said he felt badly about forgetting to read that army post card again before they started out. Last night when he went to bed he thought he would do just that, first thing in the morning.

'Don't you also feel like that, grandad?'

The old man grew wary: perhaps the lad had been looking on.

'You were awake, then?'

'I was lying down', said Györke.

A reply, much like the footpath on which they trod: a path, to be sure, but no sign of it showing anywhere underneath the snow.

They fell silent now, each going along with his own secret. Blinking, they smiled at the sparkling light and watched the sledge lest it got loose and strayed into some tricky ravine. They saw a few small birds flitting about, gathering the warmth of the morning sun; a crow caw-cawing hoarsely below them over the valley, then an eagle soaring high, its wings spread out motionless, heading for the white crags.

They came to the wood they had set out for. Old Ehedi looked for a long pole, one with a hook at its end. When he had found a suitable one they walked round the trees and where they saw dry timber, old Ehedi reached up with the pole, clamping the hook midway on the branch, and cried:

'Get out of the way, Györke!'

At a pull it would turn downward, giving a loud crack, shedding snow all over the old man who soon looked, to Györke's joy, like a walking sugar loaf. It happened, though, that in his trustful mood the old boy hooked into branches that would not give, no matter how he tugged and pulled, nor how he crept up closer at the pole's end, kicking the solid ground from under him. No matter how he grunted and trod on thin air, the big branch stood firm and would not crash down, nor even as much as creak to show at least a kindly disposition.

The old man would tug and kick a while, till he thought better of it and cried:

'Come on, Györke!'

Nimbly, Györke would be hanging on the pole before the call really had time to reach him, and along with the crashing noise they would tumble in the snow, crawl out again laughing and lick the melting snow-crystals on their lips. As if life widened out by yet another degree, they cried aloud for joy, listening with pink ears to the sound rolling out far into the white silence.

At last they had loaded up the sledge. Faggots and logs were heaped on high. They had to be fastened midway with a long rope and eased down at the top, so the many awkward bits and ends should not get across each other on the way down. Then the two generations pulled hard at it and the sledge with the big load started out for home.

They never thought they would get on so well with a huge load like that.

'If only my father could see', said Györke full of pride.

'Let it be', answered old Ehedi, 'they can do with a good man up there in the Wooded Carpathians.'

'Would Arpad have come in with the Magyars that way, grandad?'

The old man took fright in his mind for he did not rightly know the answer. After all, a poor man is a stranger to such outlying places. And the name of that confounded pass was a blank in his mind, though he had known well enough in the old days by way of which pass Arpad came into the fatherland.

'Somewhere thereabout', he said at last.

'You don't know for sure?' Györke kept pressing.

But good luck, which looks kindly upon the pure in heart, let a beautiful bird flick by.

'Look! A goldfinch!' said the old man.

And just as the Pass of Verecke was changed into a goldfinch, they reached a brook cutting its way guilelessly through the snows, softly babbling its sweet tune. 'Let's stop here', said the old man, for he wanted a drink from the brook. They stopped, and drawing a little deeper into the wood, they found a suitable place and drank. The clear spring's water refreshed them, and what they saw refreshed their eyes. For all along its course the little brook had thawed the snow along its banks and made green moss and tender leaves of grass grow. As they marvelled at the greenly winding band, they set eyes upon a deer which also drank from the brook. When it had had its fill, the young deer glanced at them, wondering what these two humans were doing here in its own quiet domain, but it didn't seem frightened at all.

'Why isn't it afraid of us, grandad?' asked Györke. The old man's face was very calm when he replied:

'The deer will know the wolf, and the people the tyrant, my boy.'

With this reassurance, they went back to the sledge and shouldering a rope each they started out again. They pulled the load slowly, for the sun had come up and shone warmly, turning the silver colour into gold. The path, too, slanted upwards, if only very gently, and as they jogged along on the whitest of grounds in the golden mellow light, one thought kept flitting through Györke's mind – what a fine soldier his father was.

'Were you never a soldier, grandad?' he asked absently.

'I was that, and more.'

'More?'

'So help me', old Ehedi said, 'for Kossuth himself, or the great

Prince Rákóczi would have slapped his knee at what I did, not merely Francis Joseph!'

Györke sensed that now his grandfather, in his life's wintertime, began to glow.

'And what was it, grandad?' he asked.

'What I did, my boy', said the old man with a sparkle in his eyes, 'was this: when I was a young lad and my brains still had wings to them to take me soaring, well, then, one Sunday morning I looked round in the world. And seeing that the great multitude of men lived in such poverty, I resolved to set this right.'

'And how did you set it right?' Györke prodded him.

'This way, my boy. I gathered the best men into a vast army, and I stood up before them and said to them: Well, fellows, this isn't right, the way the world is arranged. For he who is true is oppressed by him who is false, the hard-working man is oppressed by the thief, and the poor man by the rich. Let us take an oath that we shall wipe this blight from the earth and have in its stead a world of the just and true. Let's swear it with our minds and hoping hearts and then go to it and get it done!'

'And then?' prompted Györke.

'And then I put myself at the head of that tremendous host and, one in faith, we carried out what I said before.'

The boy looked in wonderment at his grandfather, a little alarmed, too, because he was not sure whether he dare say that something must be wrong there. But in the end he said:

'But surely, grandad, it isn't so?'

'It is so, my boy', answered the old man, 'only we do not yet know it.'

And just as old Ehedi had spoken, thus taking a plunge into the future, they reached the peak, where the path sloped gently into the far-distance. Here they stopped, by now sweating before the load. They both wiped the sweat off their foreheads and Györke said:

'And did you get no prize for it, grandad?'

'I did indeed', said the old man with pride. 'A two-fold prize even. For on the one hand I won your grandmother at that time, and on the other, I had the happy future implanted in my heart.'

The earth shone white, the sun gold.

'Let's start for home', said old Ehedi.

Both settled down on top of the pile of wood on the sledge. The old man held a strong pole in each hand, reaching down with them to the right and left of the sledge so as to steer it on the long descent, as if using a pair of rudders in that limitless sea of snow. He hardly let them touch the ground as the shank's pony sledge got moving and was soon racing down the slope.

Who knows whether they were making for home at all? Perhaps they were bound straight for the future, flying on pinions of poverty in the golden light.

c. 1946

The Spring of '45

The village woke in the morning to a mighty shock. The Russians had taken hostages.

Virág's wife ran out into the street, shaking her fists, cursing freely. Her husband, a leader of the Smallholders, a right-wing party, was one of them. Women huddled together in the doorways, wailing and blubbering. The men went hurrying to the Small-holders' party offices, or the doctor's house, almost at a trot. They gathered there, the crowd was angry and suspicious, shouting threats.

Tornyi Béni was doing his timid best to quieten them. The Russians had chosen at random, he said. There was no knowing whom they would take or leave. It might as well be himself.

'To hell with it!' one man yelled. 'Let's stand together, or else they'll carry us off one by one.' He thrust his fist up, limply.

Another did not stop there. 'Kick the Communists out of the village, they make the mischief.'

Tornyi Béni played his trump card. 'Man alive, can't you fellows see, the Russians carried off even old Katicza Kovács, and he's a regular Party member.'

This went home. There was no denying: old Kovács of the Katicza clan was a Communist, and yet the Russians had carried him off. No matter. Now was the time to speak up.

The first voice turned the argument round, carrying the crowd: 'At least, it should teach Birtalan and his like to make common cause with the Reds.' Inside the office walls of the Smallholders' the crowd felt more at ease. Peasants were thronging in, even landless peasants who in their mass supported the Peasant Party, there were even those who already had one foot in the Communist Party, not beating the drums, of course, just on the quiet. Now they patted themselves on the back for being clever. They hadn't done anything rash, like signing up with the Party.

'What kind of people are these Reds, I ask you', Sóvágó the Tall shouted at the top of his voice. 'The womenfolk can tell you . . .! Senyebikai hinted to a woman she'll get land all right if she is a bit nice to him. And *that* woman's husband is a prisoner of war!'

'Go'way, Sóvágó, Senyebikai isn't a Communist at all, he's Peasant Party.'

'What do I care –. What's the difference?' Sóvágó loathed the Peasant Party, those family black sheep, almost as much as he loathed the Reds.

Szerb Tóni was loafing near the door post, listening in. Inconspicuously, as he had come, he disappeared. He went straight to Birtalan's house.

Birtalan had a hunch that something was seriously wrong in the village. He was not keen to get to the village hall, nor to the Communist party rooms. Rather, he convinced himself that this was the day to dig up the potatoes from storage – in case the land were distributed, a good patch would have to be planted down with potatoes right away. He was crouching in the potato pit, his hands thick with clay, as he rubbed it off the potatoes. His younger son held the sacks, his elder, Péter, shouldered them and piled them up in front of the house.

'Quick, hell's loose in the village', Szerb Tóni rushed headlong into the yard.

'What's happened? What's wrong?'

'About these people the Russians carried off this morning, that's what. The Smallholders are crowding into their party office, that's where.'

'I see, I see', Birtalan mumbled, rubbing his hands with dry dust, to get them clean. 'Go with your Uncle Antal here to our Party rooms, Péter, I'll go by the backyards to Mezei's, to get the Peasant Party to move, we'll be with you in a jiffy.' And off he was.

Mezei was scraping clay from his top-boots in front of the house. He, in his turn, had dug up the mangolds that day. He was just getting ready to go to the village hall.

'We're in for it, Comrade, plague on them', said Birtalan by way of greeting.

'I know', said Mezei quietly. 'They are kicking up a shindy because of Virág and Kabai.'

'And Serfőző – so your Peasant Party should be in it, too. Only good thing is, Katicza Kovács was carried off as well. No one can say it's the Communists' doing.'

'That's just why the Russians took along old Katicza.'

'Really?'

'You bet. Both are back home already, Katicza Kovács and Serfőző. Came back last night. At Urögd they went to the pub, had quite a few drinks and on the way home they had a first-class fist fight on party-lines . . .'

Birtalan and Mezei were walking down the village main street. Women stood inside the wicket gates, looking at them from under their head-scarves with narrow eyelids, passing remarks. In their backs the two men felt the hatred of that gaze. Villás Mihály stepped up to them. He had just been to look in on his pal Katicza Kovács, but turned now to the bigger thing, the danger on the spot.

'Wouldn't it be better to call in the Russians?' he asked.

'No it wouldn't. Later, when they'll be gone, we shall still have to hold our own. Of course, at the first shot all would scurry. But this affair here isn't yet the real thing, not by far. The true defiance is within, inside the souls, or whatever you call it – ' Mezei explained. 'Better have the distribution of the land drummed out at once, and get them moving, every one of them, with stakes and spades . . .'

'What – at once?'

'At once.'

'Hm . . . But what about the squire, Kökényesdi? we haven't declared him an enemy of the people yet – '

'Who cares? We know him for what he was. Damn these – squires where you find them. He had one of his cronies, that shyster, sitting on the county council, that's why we got nowhere.'

'And what about . . . er . . . preserving the big fields in one piece?' Birtalan worried. 'Shouldn't we keep to that?'

'No. If the claimants don't want it, let them have their way. They'll learn by their own mistakes soon enough. What else can we do?'

Meanwhile it got around that two of the men whom the Russians had carried off came back home the night before, but not the two Smallholders.

'When I was called up for work on the roads', exclaimed Siket György, in the Smallholders' committee rooms 'I saw that the gentry were put to building the bridge below Ujfalu! That's where Virág and the doctor are, if you ask me!'

'When it comes to that', said Sóvágó the Tall, 'well, someone must put up the bridge, mustn't he.' He steps out of the office. Inside it was cold and dank, outside the sun is already shining strongly. He put his hands in his pockets, brooding – it's hard to find one's bearings. Without the bridge there's no getting to market, nor anything. It's not the peasants they put on repair-work, it's the gentry. And the Russians seem simply to let people off, while our own government does not . . . He cannot make head or tail of it.

He is staring idly at the water in the ditch, where stray ganders and ducks frisk about. He quacks and spits into the water. Then he moves his lips like a hare. In the meantime the village drummer had posted himself before the village hall, rolling the drum and crying:

'Notice is hereby given, that whosoever be a rightful claimant to land in the redistribution of the Csahos puszta should go out there at once, he should take with him four stakes, further a spade, or else a hoe!' The drum went tram-tram-tra-ta-ta-tram. The drummer left, walking down the road.

The village was stunned. The people were agape, struck dumb. Not half of them had seriously believed that one day the Csahos puszta would in actual fact be distributed. To them the manor was like Heaven, where you enter only after you are dead. The Claimants' Committee, the very men whose work it was, had not altogether believed that the redistribution would come about. Some had accepted membership in the Committee in case by miracle it did; some accepted membership because they would have been ashamed to refuse, ashamed of being cowards, and afraid of taking the lead. Secretly, at home, they sighed and worried at bedtime at the thought that the landlord would return and retribution follow. It would only be with luck you would escape the gallows then. That was how it happened in 1919. If you had only dared as much as go near the manor house, the gendarmes afterwards took it out on you a hundredfold. Could you expect the ways of the world to change all of a sudden, right now? Further, they accepted membership, convinced, that nothing would come of the whole thing anyway. By the time they got started, the county administration would stop them from going ahead, the squire would return, black horses and all, same way as he left. Black carriage, black horses . . . Further, they accepted membership in case the village needed martyrs. They'd be the martyrs. The grandchildren, at least, would then recall their memories. They had spent weeks on end assessing and computing, comparing strips, walking the fields, adjudging the claimants, pondering who had a right to land and who hadn't, without ever believing that they would really and truly parcel out the puszta. All told, about half the Committee might have believed it. People like Villás

Mihály went the whole hog, cultivation in common, and all, because at heart they didn't believe in it. Such people mostly became Communists because they yearned to be something wholly different from what a villager is. Not very far from the Robin Hoods of old, who broke away from everything that stood for the deadly stultification of village life. A Communist, then, in their eyes, is the man who is at war with all that is of the present and all that is of the past – faith, ethics, custom, the idea of private property. To accomplish an act, at long last, so that all stifled passion, all the quenched impulses break loose, the tempest rages! Now they are trooping out towards the puszta, gay, wide-awake, marching as into a wilderness, with the spades like muskets in their hands. They'll teach them – out there they'll pick off the gentry. In their eyes the squire is the gentry personified. All the others, like the German lessee, the county administrator, the town-clerk, the gendarmes are swarming around, seen far away, as through a haze. The people of the village have as good as grown up on these fields and pastures, and so have their fathers and grandfathers, on day labour, weeding, hoeing, harvesting, trench-digging, beet digging, corn husking and every manner of labour there is in the fields. They know every bend and fold of the manor, every ditch, meadow, marsh, tree and track – the very rainbows arise again at the thought of how the downpours chased them from their days' earnings. Bawlings, scoldings, cursings keep quivering in the air, immutably. Memories crop up of savage, infamous overseers, of blackguardly bailiffs and stewards, of peasants swollen-headed with their office, as they became farm foremen, head shepherds, field-guards. The wind, as they go along, carries the long faded songs of their youth, the manor like a piercing memory, widens out in fancy crescents. Crescent of the park. Of the acacia grove. Of the ancient shaggy-leafed trees around the pig-pens, the swine-herds' hutments. The light is creased on the drooping roof of the cow-house, the hired men's whips coil on and on in the air, holding back the crack, like belated snakes in the leafmould, oh, the staggering past this place has, Heavenly Father! It knows of the early morning's anguish, – who will be taken on for day-labour and who won't – and the Saturday night's jitters, did the week's wages go up or down? On this manor old Sóvágó, the tall Sóvágó's father who cracked up with overwork, died. Here Szomoru Klára was got with child. She sued the overseer but since he was penniless, she drowned the child and herself. On this manor their lordships spent their lives as the high and mighty. A broad, surging stream of life that carried generations of gentry-folk upon its billowing surface, brought them on like drift-wood and set them here ashore. At one time a Count from Tran-sylvania, having squandered his fortune, lived here as a permanent guest. Getting rid of his riches had made a poet of him. The things this place has seen, Father in Heaven! Here an old hired man lost his right eye when they were getting in the hay. A weed had got into it in the morning, the bailiff did not let him off to see the doctor, by evening he could not see any more. A week after there was nothing for it but to remove his eye at the hospital. And what of the untold mean vexations? Here the peasant was made to pay a florin if his horse happened to nibble at a gourd, here, yes here the village that stood from the beginning of time was shedding its sweat and anguish on the fields and meadows. Not a field without a story to it. Life and all that makes for it flocked together here. As though the village and its houses were not more than a resting place for the night. Here they were treading out the corn with horses, winnowing in the wind, before there were threshing machines. Here the harvesters in the late summer worked for their share in the crop, here their earnings were dealt out in brandy, lard and wheat, here the sickness crept into the chest of the girls carrying chaff. Here the pick of the village girls fell to the overseers, to the lords of the manor – ho, there's no end to what happened around here. (Who among you, fellow-writers, shall write one day the true and candid story of Hungary's latifundia?)

Right now, however, these people, former estate servants, former day labourers, share-croppers and hired men were on their way to divide up the manorial land among themselves.

The Claimants' Committee went in front, not in file, or any set manner, Birtalan and Mezei being first, – with Mezei half a step in front – and the rest following in a group. The Claimants after them, in even greater confusion, thronging together at random. Some straggled at hollering distance, others, again, were trying out the way in every manner, in case it was better there than here. They jumped the ditch, walking on the grassy bank, they ran into puddles, and leaped back over the ditch, walking along for a while with the rest, till they branched off again, this time to the other side.

There is something profoundly human in these people's different ways, not accepting what all the rest accept. They want to arrive where the crowd, the great majority is going, but they want to go differently, and what's more, to arrive differently. As if they had assumed, from the very first that this dealing out of the land cannot be something final and definitive, that they shall be called to account. Then they could always point out that even though they did go out to the manor lands with the rest, they did not go quite the same way.

There always had been such wary peasant ways, at all times and occasions, but they were never so much in evidence. Nor could they be. Never yet had the villagers come so near to distributing the manor land.

'We'll stop when we get in front of the manor house, mates, and draw lots!' Birtalan cried, turning round, after which he changed step and pushed on.

Those few who were looking for the better way off the road got themselves into a marshy stretch of grassland, and tried to hurry out, by leaps and quick spurts. They have been taught again, what they've known all along, of course, that meadows are treacherous, they look so smooth and friendly from a distance, till something splashes under your foot, yet you go on and on, you think you'll get soon to the end. By the time it dawns on you, you are right in the bog, and there's no going backwards or forwards. But they'll do it all the same, just to stand aside, they won't learn the lesson, not on your life.

The sun has crept higher, the meadows stretch away in a mass of green, the mud dries up, the villagers have reached the double row of huge acacia trees, with the arable land lying to right and left.

'If it were for me, I'd pick my land just here,' says Szerb Tóni. He stops short and lets his eye slide along the bend of the ploughed field, judiciously. 'That's where I'd build up my home, on the edge of the grazing grounds. Pigs and sheep could run loose, and as soon as you unyoke your oxen, you can drive them out. . .'

'You'll have your land, mate, where the dice fall for you', another shouted at him, a little scornfully. After all, Szerb Tóni was a mere newcomer to the village.

The road, running between the acacia rows, was broadening out. The last of the landowners wanted to live up to the reputation of the first and had kept this road in trim. After every rainfall he had it harrowed. In time it smoothed over, as if it were concrete. The acacias were a hundred years old, or more, they were thick-set, black and rugged. Long gone is the bailiff who had them planted. And gone the labourers or bondmen who dug the ditch.

'Look, mate, lots of wood for grave-posts . . .' one of the men said to his neighbour.

'Lots. But they'd make carved gate posts as well.'

'They would. And sledges too, and carts.'

At a distance someone echoed:

'A cart made from acacia wood lasts you for a lifetime . . .'

The trees in the row changed shape in their minds, becoming sledges, carts, gateposts.

There are worlds for each man to choose from as he walks along – imagination runs riot along the width of the road. The road, traced out for communication by the French knight-errant Monsieur Monpensier in the dim beginning; the road on which bondsmen in their hundreds, thousands, and tens of thousands trod to do corvée and pay tithes to the domain during the centuries of oppression; the road where the Emperor Leopold's henchmen galloped to lay hands on the county family's scion that sided with the insurgents. The road where high life rolled along in coach-and-sixes in the glamorous 'nineties, when the Counts Tisza and the drawing-room favourites among the writers went backwards and forwards visiting. Where the last of the livery coachmen, Gulyás Lajos was taking the lady of the manor, – by that time only with four-in-hand – and they quarrelled on the way. The lady was nagging – 'what kind of driving is that, Lajos?' And Lajos pulled the reins, the foursome came to a halt, Lajos jumped off the driver's seat, and said if her ladyship knows better, she should do her own driving. And he left her halfway between the village and the manor. As well he might. It was in the year 'nineteen, and he was the estate servants' shop steward. There's no end to what this road has seen. At certain hours of the night and day gendarmes came and went in pairs, guarding the manor house. Ox-carts rattled along the road morning and evening, droves of cattle were sent from one end of the estate to the other, – a highway for swineherds, flocks of sheep, cowherds, livestock, bondsmen and gentlefolk.

The road runs straight up to the wrought-iron gates of the park. Above the gates rusty iron ornaments hug an electric bulb. The estate had its own electric plant, but it broke down. Some bulbs are still left and urchins shoot at them with pebbles. Next to the gate there is an acacia grove to the right and one to the left. On this side are the stables on that side the estate servants' yard. An open space lies between the stables and the woods, and the farmyard edges up to the wood with the pig-sties. Memories, stories . . . and every single one of them had at one time stood under those eaves, weathering a downpour or a storm.

The wrought-iron gates, however, are now hanging loose on

broken hinges. Inside, lies the park, with its pines, birches, acacias, oaks, maples, alders and all sorts of trees. Some had grown wild, others had been planted by this lord or that bailiff. A maze of winding paths is set out under the trees, skirting the groves, thickets and hedges. The last owner was no longer able to carry the expense of the upkeep, and to preserve it in all its glory. He tried to have a few things done, here and there.

But meanwhile the people have crowded in thick groups in front of the manor house.

All the inhabitants, Mademoiselle Mélanie, Posz Bálint the farm foreman, Csorba Győző the agent and the poultry breeder Varga János came flocking out into the porch. Not having had anything better to do, they had been playing cards for pumpkin seeds all morning. They were staring at the crowd, bewildered.

'Heaven help us, they're carving up the land . . .!' Mademoiselle Mélanie is whispering. She is deaf, and so her voice comes in a thin falsetto.

'It seems they are', the agent muttered, turning pale at the thought of the five thousand odd pengös the estate owed him. No estate, no getting back his money. The poultry breeder is aloof: something at least is going to happen in this hole, it had been dull enough since the war. He had a house in the village, and a patch of land, grown-up daughters, a wife . . . what can happen? If the worst came to the worst, he'd be stationed again near the pub, in the village, worse luck. But as for Posz Bálint, he is thunderstruck. What cattle there remained on the estate he had taken under his wings, and as time passed, he had come more and more to regard them as his own. Land, too, he carved out a fair patch for himself. He sowed down a good deal of it in the autumn, and he had already ploughed up as much as his laziness would let him . . . He turned and headed straight for home – the stables, that is.

'What's the hurry, you there!' one of the villagers cried after him, 'we'll take away the cattle anyhow', but Birtalan quietens him down: 'Leave him alone. At least he's tending the animals. Posz has three horses in the stable, two oxen, four breeding sows and a mangy piglet. And all out of the estate!'

'Come on, come on!' Senyebikai urges them.

In a manner of speaking they were drawing nearer, but you could tell which ones did not care to stand to the fore. Not everybody believed in the distribution of the estate, not even at this hour. They only came along just in case – you can never tell.

'Now listen to me, Comrades!' Birtalan flared up. 'First of all we are going to draw lots for the part of the estate we shall distribute first; then for the names – whose land is to be first in the field in question, whose next, and so on. The "dice" were prepared by the Claimant's Committee – there are "dice" for each part of the estate, and for each individual claimant. We shall put them all in a hat, and each of you shall take out one and hold it up. Let's begin. Give me a hat, someone.'

Five or six of the men whipped off their hats and offered them. They stood bare-headed, keyed up.

'Well then, first we draw lots for the location – which part of the estate to start on . . .' and he reached for one of the hats, at random.

Senyebikai, in a fluster, dived into his pockets, looking for the dice, and threw them into the hat.

'There! Take one out, somebody.'

The lot fell on the Ladies' Dell.

The Ladies' Dell stretched off the north-eastern corner of the park, towards the road to Várad. Senyebikai went in front, with the measuring chain on his shoulder. The villagers glanced back towards the manor house and thronged after him.

'This is where the first stake goes down', he said, taking in with his eye the width of the grassy strip between the ditch that en-circles the orchard and the edge of the ploughed field. The manor house was no longer visible behind the trees. Something oppressive had wrenched itself from the crowd, something that was still with them in sight of the manor. Now they see only the trees beyond the ditch, the expanse of the fields before them and the wider expanse of the sky, blue with all the blues of Spring. In the far distance, dark patches show on the sky-line, villages. Others perhaps are standing there, as they themselves are here, along a farm track, shaking in an old hat, the tiny folded pieces of paper with names written on them.

People stood patiently in a row along the dirt road, as though they were reluctant to tread on the soaked clods of the ploughed land. They stood on the grassy banks of the ditch as well, and even right in the ditch. One was rubbing off the leafmould from his boots; another staring at the hat in Villás Mihály's hand, wondering on whom chance was going to smile – you dip your hand into that hat and you pull out a number, and that number will tell what kind of land will be yours. Your own hand will bring bad or good fortune.

'Listen, mates!' Senyebikai said all of a sudden. He had a flair for history. 'Before we get going with casting the lot, it wouldn't hurt to give a thought to this: that the land which the dice are about to allot us, well, it was bestowed on us by the Peasant Party.' That was too much by half for Katicza Kovács.

'Strike me dead!' he cried, 'and where do we come in, we Communists? If it weren't for us, d'you think any living soul would get as much as a single furrow?'

The men came alive slowly, like water flowing over in a ditch. The Smallholders too began to remember their party allegiance, like an itch on the skin. One of them said this, the other that. Birtalan was gazing at the uproar, on the crowd, and at each man in turn. As though at each man's side, as a shadow, his past was standing to attention. There were hard fighters amongst them, experienced men who had gone through many sufferings from their early youth to this day, standing up for ideals like the secret ballot, and 'the land to him that works it', . . . and 'one sheep-fold, one shepherd' . . . for every fighting word and marching song of the long-gone Springs, when they had made a bid for human dignity, indeed, for being socialists. At least once in a while, around the First of May, when the bitterness of poverty and the inhumanity of life were cutting deepest. Here is Senyebikai, and he was of the best, an old fighter, though now he speaks another language . . . And the others, Fakó Ferenc, and that nice old Katicza Kovács, what have they stood up to and suffered in the bygone days, to come to rest at long last, here on the corner of the Ladies' Dell dirt road on the bank of the ditch. And suddenly he feels that for his part he must speak of two men.

'Let's quiet down a bit, Comrades', he said. 'What sense is there now in quarrelling among ourselves? We've got the land, that is for sure and no one can take it away from us. I grant you that the Peasant Party has got its share in giving us the land, but you should not forget, mates, that the man in the government who dispenses the land is called Nagy Imre! And as to his party, he's a Communist. But as things have come to such a pitch, that I am forced to refer to my own party, I will say yet another man's name, and that will be – Rákosi Mátyás.' He drew in the smoke from his cigarette end violently, chucked it away and pushed his cigarette-holder into his trouser pocket. He was now hard as a rock. He glanced at the men. 'I didn't mean to brag. But since I named him, you comrades might at least touch your hats, even if you don't say nothing.'

Katicza Kovács wrenched his crumpled hat from his head, others too, touched their hats, there's no denying, but many tried to have their cake and eat it. That is to say, the Smallholders were looking at Birtalan as if they too had touched their hats.

Birtalan smiled faintly, then said:

'And now, let's get on with it . . . where are those paper chits?'

Villás Mihály was holding the hat by its brim with both hands, he even shut his eyes, so no one should suspect him.

'Someone pull out the first slip . . . someone that didn't have his finger in the pie last night! he cried.

'That's me, haw-haw,' Katicza Kovács laughed aloud, and turning his head to one side, he rummaged with his hand in the hat. He pulled out a folded chit, opened it and reeled as he read it out aloud: 'Sóvágó Károly!'

The tall Sóvágó was loafing well to the rear. He hit the ground with his spade, pulled a wry face and trudged to the front. He swallowed his tongue, one thing was certain – he did not run down the Communists. All eyes looked at him. Why of all people should he be in such luck? He wasn't in any way a democrat, he was an enemy not only of the Communists but of all who wanted to see a new world in place of the old. But luck does not go by deserts, it comes to you, blindly . . .

'Drive down a stake right here, Károly . . . and write your name upon it . . . or have you written it already?' Senybikai made a mark with his heel in the soft upturned sod, and stepped aside, He undid the measuring chain.

The tall Sóvágó fitted his stake to the assigned spot, dourly. He had written his name on the stake already at home. Now he was patting down the post with the butt-end of his spade.

'Step aside, mate', Árkus Jóska cried, in a big way, since he had a hatchet. He came down on the post with a mighty swing that sent it into the ground a spit deep. The bang raised an echo down the park, it vibrated among the trees, broke as it reached the manor house, went limp against its walls, like a spent gust of wind.

Birtalan fumbled with a sheet of paper, looking up the tall Sóvágó's name on the list.

'Ten and one half cadastral yokes',* he announced, 'by reason of the tall Sóvágo having four children.'

Senyebikai slipped one end of the measuring chain into Sóvágó's hand, he himself set out at a trot with the other end along the dirt road. Mezei walked in the middle of the road, with paper and

* The yoke is one and a third acres.

pencil, working out the area in yokes from the number of metres to the frontage. Villás Mihály made ready for another drawing of lots, quietly cursing Sóvágó, for he would have fancied the corner plot for his own . . . Soon another post was driven in with bangs along the track, the belated echo rolled down the rear, the men began to fan out. They got their land. More men had gathered near the new stakes. As time passed, only a few remained. The ones who were first to get their land were stepping it out lengthwise. The rest were lost to sight as they proceeded along the track, like members of a dispersing army on the land that lay thrown open in its immensity –

From Chapter 37 of Isten malmai (The Mills of God).

1949

The Test

I

Sunday morning at the co-operative farm they were discussing the harvest. The Government decree had come: the grain must be reaped waxripe. On the fields you could already see shocks here and there. Borsos Lajos glimpsed whole rows on the Szikhát. Maybe it was rye or autumn barley, it didn't matter; when people see corn standing in shocks, they get harvest-fever, start reaping, in case the grain drops away or hail or fire destroys it.

Those who worked at Balószeg, on the Co-op fields, gathering alfalfa, hoeing maize, couldn't agree. One said the wheat was still green, another that you could start at Tarka-row, where the rye was blanching on the patches of sodic soil. They asked the supervisor, too, who lived on the farmstead, seeing the fields every day; but he wouldn't risk a straight reply, either. In certain spots, he said, the grain was yellowing; but the ears were still milky. Then he held forth on how it was when he served the lords of Patkos, what tender wheat they cut.

But of what use were empty words? Let the Co-op leaders survey all the fields.

A leader even among leaders, chairman Sós Mihály was around sixty, but still in good shape. Formerly a tenant farmer on 20 yokes, he had to know something about farming; which was why they chose him. Few realized however that Aunt Zsuzsi was the real farmer. It was a well kept secret. Everyone has a picture of himself for the outside world, for others to see on the village square, at church, taverns, party-councils, and there is also a true one only the people at home know.

The other top committee member, Csapó Bandi – he'd stay Bandi all his born days – was a carter and new holder. Alert, fast talker, glib liar, in the thick of everything from the first – that's how he got ahead in the Co-op, too. He started to organize it, so he could not be left out; that wouldn't have been fair. Whoever starts something should have the first word. Otherwise, a Jack-of-all-trades, he'd tried his hand as an itinerant worker, hawker, rabbit skinner, barkeeper . . . only land he'd never had, not even to spit on. Finally he wound up at carting. With the aid of two poor horses and some hefty, teen-age sons, he carted stone on the highway, coal and wood from the railway station, grain for the Co-op, now this, now that.

The third leader was Kis Gábor, a former farmhand and share-cropper. He'd always lived off someone else's land, the most he ever worked himself was a patch of potatoes. He used to raise beet and maize for the big landowners, for a third and fourth share.

They set out early next morning, even before dawn, to survey the fields. Let no one say: the Co-op leaders rise late! They knew a thousand jealous eyes kept watch.

They went there by cart; Balószeg being about a two hours walk, and none of them so young any more. The cart wasn't the Co-op's, but Csapo Bandi's, since the Co-op's few teams were busy with the corn and alfalfa. Just before harvest everything must be in order. Maize needs hoeing, alfalfa must be cut and stacked up; no one would have time later. This was the main thing now. The Co-op's teams could not be used for hauling a few men. Should anyone bring horses in from the fields for that reason, the leaders would never hear the end of it.

Going home from the meeting, Csapó Bandi had said, 'Look Mihály, there is no problem; I'll hitch up. I was planning to take a look at the children's little wheat-patch anyway.' (It wasn't the childrens' but his own, but no one need know. Better be on the safe side!)

Kis Gábor didn't like the offer. He'd rather have walked, having no bicycle yet. Such things never end well. The free work would be brought up later. Even the seemingly purest favour burps up after the second shot of brandy, or third glass of wine, and calculated favours certainly were apt to come high. But he'd blush before the other members to have to put in the big book: so and so much transportation so the leaders could see the wheat.

Since he was a man who thought before he spoke, while he was thinking, the others decided. They would start the next morning at 3.30 a.m. from the far end of the village, by Maurer's Mill, let everyone be there. By then he couldn't very well say no, he'd rather walk; that would hurt the feelings of the older men. They might think he meant, I'm a better man, a good Socialist, and that he looked down on others. That would be bad. They'd just started to work together, peace should be kept at any price. If you fight on your own, not many notice; but if there is strife in the Co-op, the whole village laughs. Even in marriage, you start out with: 'I'll go half way, and you too: then, we'll get along somehow.' So Kis Gábor kept silent while they discussed details, since he was too late to speak. He was there next morning to get the free ride. We shouldn't be too proud, even of our own honesty. That can bring anger, too. He didn't pursue this thought all the way, but it coloured his feeling of annoyance.

When they arrived, they themselves could see it wasn't easy to decide. The fields sparkled with all the hues of near-harvest time. Next to dark green maize, faded green potatoes, and live-green beets, were milky-yellow barley, wan-white rye, golden wheat greenish-yellow oats, even on the lands of private owners. On the Co-op fields even the same crop had different colours, depending on who had that piece of land last year, what grew on it, when it was manured, when ploughed. Across the wheat fields multi-coloured patches showed the signs of the last owner's care. Those who last season – when they worked it on their own – ploughed deep, already had golden wheat. The ones who hoed their maize just twice, had only a green crop, and those who left the soil untended in the autumn just had faded pale wheat.

The committee scanned the fields in turn, feeling, tasting the ears. Sós Mihály mumbled glumly that the ears were too soft, too milky, some yellow, others still green. The spring-sowing was not yet ripe. He couldn't help thinking that if it were his own he'd say, let it wait a few more days. Wheat sometimes ripens fast, in a day or two, yet may also take a whole week. You've got to look at it day by day. If it were mine, I wouldn't start yet – only when the grain cracks under your teeth. 'This is soft dough yet,' he kept saying. 'Wheat is best when it yellows slowly, then it keeps. It fills up then and hardens; though, Devil knows how, once I had a wheat crop, all green, when along came a hot wind, and, as I watched, in two days all was ripe. Had to start reaping straight off in case the grain scattered. Still I got more than a long ton per acre.' That's how Sós Mihály went on, crumbling fresh wheat grains with his fingers. Csapó prettied up his hat with the bending ears.

Kis Gábor added quietly: 'It could be, Mihály, that your yield was more than a ton; but, if not for the heat, it could have been thirty per cent higher.

'Maybe so', he answered. 'We had about thirty shocks per acre, but only ninety pounds of grain in most of them, though the shocks were big, and the straw tall. This high', he added, showing that the wheat came to his chin.

They sized up through all of the Balószeg lots, then those at Haromnyárfás, – arguing, explaining, but couldn't agree when to call all the members to the harvest line.

Sós Mihály was afraid of responsibility, didn't dare decide. He was now more leery of Co-op members, the Party, Commonalty, Government and All Powers That Be than earlier he had been of his wife, who blamed him if he started work early, blamed him if he delayed; argued if he sold livestock at the fair, scolded if he didn't.

Csapó Bandi didn't know much about farming – never had anything to do with it. Now he'd say, 'It's ready for the scythe . . .' then again, 'Could take a week yet!' As even the song puts it, 'First the wheat must ripen . . .'

Kis Gábor, as usual, kept silent, thinking. Then, as they paused at the end of a big field, to decide what to report – after all if they couldn't get the thing straight even among themselves, they'd be a laughing stock! – he finally spoke:

'Listen, Bandi. Look, Mihály! This here wheat, in our first Co-op year, is so motley, showing the varying care of former owners. I've harvested many summers at the Count's, at the Monastery, and for Schlesinger, too. I know what wax-ripe is. Sometimes, at the start, we almost dropped in our tracks – cutting the raw stalks was so hard. It was yellow, yet still tough. But in the stacks it grew ripe, reddish and like steel! Our crop isn't like that yet. We could glean some ripe rows, but it's not worth it. We can't bring out twenty-four hands to scout for ripe rows here and there. I'd say, we'll have to come out again, and when most of it is ripe, worth starting on, then let's call the members. The rest of the crop will ripen to the scythe. That's how it used to be on the Estate.'

Sós Mihály was ashamed it wasn't he who had spoken the last word, as called for – but Gábor was right. The leaders should not just talk, they should reach an agreement.

Csapó Bandi concurred, his mind being on something else, anyway, namely on how could he stow some of the Co-op's alfalfa in his wagon, at least enough for a few feedings. As they walked, he unbridled the horses, so they could browse on ears of wheat or purslane on the roadside. When he saw alfalfa cut and drying in the row, he would toss a pitchforkful for the horses to munch, while they conferred. When they drove on, he thriftily put the leftovers in the wagon. At other stops he again foraged for them. Nothing so gladdens a carter as to see his horses get a bite of someone else's feed. All his life, driving through the fields, he used to throw a few forkfuls of hay, a bunch of alfalfa, some buckwheat, oats, a few gourds, beets, or ears of corn onto his wagon – whatever he came across. He still did. Before they started home, he got out the pitch-fork again. Let those poor horses have a snack for giving the Com-mittee a ride. Sós Mihály didn't even notice, he was used to it from the old days. The leader's horses, passing the fields, were always eating someone else's hay. But Kis Gábor looked at the bared patches as if they were pulling his teeth. He just kept looking, without a word, but Csapó Bandi felt the sharp eyes and stirring anger; so he didn't dare gather more, and, as he brought his haul to the wagon, he blinked apologetically, saying to Kis Gábor: 'These poor beasts couldn't eat at dawn, because my sons, the rascals, were at a ball till morning.'

2

Sós Mihály led the first team of reapers, Csapó Bandi the second, Kis Gábor the third. The men were just warming to each other, and to the job. You couldn't rush: not the cutting (it was still wet below), not the binding (you had to let the sheaves dry), nor the shocking (in case the crop get mildew, or the wheat grew musty, the chaff bitter, and the animals refused it). But harvesting seems to drive people. It is such a joy, such a thrill to see the win-drows fall before the scythe, the full sheaves roll, the stacks gather. So Sós Mihály urged in vain: 'Don't push so hard, men, we have time . . .' Before they knew it, they were driving on again.

Meanwhile each scanned the others' work, compared it with his own. Who reaped how, was his row too narrow, his stubble too high, did his scythe scatter the wheat, leaving some stalks behind, was the row straight, were the sheaves neat (not too long at the stock, loose in binding)? That's what eyes, narrowed by the rilling salt sweat, searched for. When they got to the end of a long row, the smokers lighted up. Then, with clenched pipe, or a cigarette sticking to one side of their mouths – carrying the scythe on their shoulders, sharp side down, or under their arms, sharp side up – secretly they estimated whether others cheated or got out of step. One spied if the next row were narrower than his own. The other, if his own were the narrower. The good hands strove not to work less than others; the sly ones sought to hedge, if possible. The honest ones matched their row with the best – the sly ones with the worst. They wouldn't work a stroke more than they must. So far there was no talk or even conscious thought about this; such things just crop up, brought on by work and human nature.

The first rift came in Sós Mihály's team. Bull-like Major Béni, Sós Mihály's nephew (and reaping just behind him), with his forty-four inch scythe and his long legs cut a bigger swath than the others, just to show off. There were also weaker members in the team, too, who could not be driven too hard. One was sickly, another blighted by poverty, a third, somewhat elderly, would be able to work well by himself for years yet but found it hard to keep up with the others. The fourth hand was Szabó Miska, a youngster and tyro, who took the place of his sick father. He didn't know yet how to hammer or sharpen the scythe, or how to reap. From many points, many households, came the members; only here, side by side, would they know who was who.

Béni, going back for a fresh start, gave the rows of the other reapers an over-critical look, sometimes even checking to see if they were a full six feet wide.

Nothing happened, though, on the first day. Only slight whispers as evening approached, when most of the men were tired out. The first day of harvest wears out even those who work every day. Each task requires a different kind of strength, uses of other muscles. Those who felt strong and fit, swapped glances, as if saying: why should anyone join the Co-op if he can't keep up?

The second day, around noon – when even the usual small vagrant clouds failed to check the heat – just as they were cutting raw-stemmed rye, which climbed the scythe handles of the less experienced, Major Béni erupted with pride and jumped Szabó Miska: 'Son, where did you learn to reap?' The poor boy, as anxious over the job as a hungry calf at his mother's udder, didn't even dare lift his eyes from his work, or wipe the perspiration with his sleeve, for even that would mean a scythe-swing less; so, from his brow, his eyelashes, the tip of his nose, from his chin and neck, dripped soiled sweat. He glanced abashed at his huge partner.

'Back home', he answered quietly.

'Well, tell your father to teach you to reap before he sends you in his place. You'll be to blame if we lose the clean-stubble contest. In your rows even a six-week-old piglet could hide!'

The lecture was for Miska, but others could grasp it too, and did, in chagrin (it was well enough for those with so much God-given strength) mixed with secret shame: why, or why did I come here, to be among such conceited men as this ox of a Béni. Only one reaper, old Tóth, Miska's uncle, put in a word for the boy, just mildly, old-man like: 'All right, Béni, you were eighteen once too. No one learns this in his mother's womb . . .'

Béni was just waiting to snap back: 'When I was eighteen, I outdid the first reaper, though I was hired only as a sheaf-binder.'

Sós Mihály said nothing, although it was his duty to settle the matter. But he was aging, too; work was hard for him, and he'd never harvested in a team before. His rows were not faultless. He had to cope with a worn scythe, narrowed to an inch's width, since Aunt Zsuzsi would give him no money for a new one. 'Blast your Co-op', she said, 'This scythe was good enough till now. Let them give you a new one, if this won't do. I shan't spend on it, never saw any sense to this Co-op business anyhow, is just a lot of talk and meetings.' Uncle Mihály chose to keep still. The point of his scythe bent towards the ground, for its middle was giving way. He had to hold it up a little, in case the president's scythe should break in the row. What a disgrace! He had to reap a bit shallow, leaving higher stalks. He wasn't the one to take issue, whose scythe left such a mark that even on bare stubble you could track it, till the tractors turned it in. Besides, Major Béni was his nephew, old Tóth his kin, the Szabó boy's father an old friend – that's the reason they were here. Whichever finger he bit would hurt.

Luckily they were nearing the start of a new row and Béni, with a last snort – saying: 'I won't work for others, earn for others' – took out his anger on the tough rye, and, just for spite, cut an even wider swath.

At the same time, a fight broke out in Csapó Bandi's team; not over the work, but the water. A bad mood had already poisoned the air. The waterboy, Teleki Jancsi, couldn't keep up with the demand, for they all drank by the pitcherful. The silly lad, not for spite but through inexperience, always started with the first reaper, and, since, everyone drank in each row, none was left for those in back. The sun blazed; the raw, hard rye parboiled the men, their palates dried out; they were ready to drop. So, as the water-boy each time began at the head of the rows, those in the back broke out swearing.

'Damn you, brat, I'll dip my scythe in you if you take the water up front again!' That's what Tóth Jankó, the last reaper, yelled, and poked scorn at Csapó Bandi: 'You can see he's a carter, a rabbit-skinner; he can't keep order. Then why is he first reaper?

Let him come back here, let him stew, and he'll learn how many yards reach how long!'

Only Kis Gábor handled things right. He advanced with quiet firmness, careful not to lag behind the other teams, rather forging ahead a bit – always keeping an eye on his men. He also told the waterboy: 'You started here last time, son. Now go to the back, or they'll never get fresh water!' If one of the reapers or sheaf-binders muffed his work, he'd stop a while, in passing, and look at it, but not long enough to attract the others' attention. He might drop a word, like: 'Your whetstone is bad.' (The man would welcome an excuse: 'No good at all; confound that shopkeeper who sold me it!') Or maybe he'd say: 'Your scythe is angled too wide. That factory-made key is to blame. There's nothing can beat the old-style wedge!' This way the man would correct his work, give his utmost. Kis Gábor knew alert, keen eyes availed more than scolding words. He kept the speed in check too. Mornings, right after hammering, with freshly sharpened scythes he'd push on a little, but never dispersed them. He let no one lag. If someone was stronger than the rest, and, to show off, cut a wider swath, went faster and pressed the one in front, he'd tell him, out of the others' earshot: 'Don't strain son, let the others catch up!' Some on his team were strong and tough, like Mihályi Ferenc. He started to grumble about others cutting smaller rows. Kis Gábor told him: 'Look, Ferenc, if you can do more than others, fine, but you needn't take it out on the rest of the team. Don't make broader rows than others, if you don't want to. Everyone can stand the norm, even a little more. We must keep order, we won't kill each other, like we used to in the olden days, on the stubble of the big estates. Understand? And don't start an argument here; it will only lead to trouble. Then we'll have to go before the Party.'

At lunchtime, when the women came from the village with their basins of food and satchels, the sheaf-binding girls – all daughters of the members – while their fathers napped, filled in their mothers with the news: what were the problems, who was what kind of a man – Major Béni arrogant, Csapó Bandi a sly, insufferable blowhard, Csiri Borsos a tobacco chewer (whoever drank after him got mouth sores). The president, old Sós, was a weakling who couldn't keep order; nobody listened to, or respected, him; his team was always quarrelling – the same with Csapó's team. Csiri Borsos, the small, black-haired, bandy-legged tobacco chewer had tangled with big-mouthed Tóth Jankó, who resented being last reaper, and Csiri Borsos, whose nickname *Csiri* referred to his small stature, ran at him with his scythe, ready to slice off his head – 'Wouldn't scare me', he said, 'if he were twice as big' – and probably would have done it, too, if the others hadn't held him back. He really was a wild one. Seems Tóth Jankó once said to him (when Csapó wasn't there, and Csiri Borsos, taking his place as first reaper, told him off), 'Who are you to order us around here anyway? An acorn worm, a pipe-cud! I'll kick you so hard, you'll bump the old sun from the sky!' If Uncle Kis Gábor, close by with his men, hadn't stepped between them, it could have led to murder. Yes, Uncle Kis Gábor was a good man; it was fine to be with his team, where there was always singing and joking, but the work got done, too. 'Here, in our teams, there is constant bickering and fighting' – that's what the girls from the Sós and Csapó groups were saying. The women spread the news in the whole village. Back home, by the well, under windows, at the mill and village square, they passed judgment on the Balószeg Co-op and all its ills. Szabó Miska's mother, learning what Major Béni told her son, cursed him out before a large group of women; might that ox collapse, for all his strength, lose it forever; even in getting to bed may he have to crawl on hands and knees; let the Good Lord make him too weak to pull up his own pants, if he was so jealous of her son, sent in place of a sick husband.

But when the going was easier, folks turned gay and forgot their flashing anger. In ending a shift, as the teams neared, friends would shout across at each other. Varga Imre, from the second team, yelled to Szabó Erzsi, his nightly dancing partner in the third team, as she bent over in work, flashing her pretty legs: 'Say, Erzsi, you're showing your . . .' then went on in song, 'I'll buy a kerchief for my sweetheart . . .' And she yelled back: 'Words don't reach from over there, Varga Imre, you're a bear.'

'Why the racket, don't you hear how nicely I sing?' joshed Imre in reply. To Csiri Borsos, Kis Gábor shouted: 'Here, old Pal, have a cud, sweet as sugar!'

In the evenings, all three teams assembled. The younger ones even sang and danced in a corner of the stubble, after a bacon fry. The older ones sat together to talk, in two or three mixed groups, not by teams. They discussed politics, criticized the village Co-op leaders, tried to gauge the yield, spoke of what should be done next year in the Co-op to have things better.

By now they all knew Sós Mihály was weak, Csapó Bandi crooked. Csapó got away with everything. Facing a new field, with good smooth ground and easy cutting, he'd keep still; but if the wheat were leaning or matted, he'd say, 'Let's draw lots', it was unfair to keep giving him the tough parts. That was false, of course; others got bad breaks too, but he was full of guile. If the crop were light and sparse, he'd tell the girls to bind smaller sheaves, so they'd have the same number as the rest. Mornings, when they wove binders – all three teams together – he'd brag that his team made most. But he told his daughter to put only fourteen or fifteen binders in a pile, instead of the usual eighteen. That would be noticed only later, at work, when they'd miss a binder for a sheaf here and there. That's why it was decided that each team should use their own binders. If they cheated, they'd be cheating themselves. But the main reason men fumed at Csapó was for his way of always slacking. If old Sós said he'd have to look over the acreage to see where to start tomorrow, or if the location of the shifts had to be set in advance, Csapó insisted that Sós not go alone. He'd try to have Kis Gábor go, too; that was the democratic way – just so he could shirk a while. He'd always seek to promote such things as field scanning, shift choosing, shock counting, or surveys of corn, alfalfa or livestock, at the hottest time of day, or when the next batch of wheat was leaning or matted. Even his own team was angry at him. On tough jobs he always found some excuse to leave them. If he hadn't feared Kis Gábor, he would have idled away the whole day, cooling under the trees, visiting the tavern, just as the foremen of olden days used to do, going back on any pretext to the farm or village, swilling beer at the inn, while the men swallowed dry in the heat of the day, often lacking even fresh water. If that sly Csapó could think of nothing else, he'd feign a bellyache, resting his scythe again and again. Even his half-grown daughter, Sári, who fooled with boys till dawn, but used to fall asleep at binder-weaving and, when told, 'Sweet dreams, Sári!' would snap back viciously – even she was spared by him. When he went off somewhere, Sári would sit at the end of the row instead of binding, or lending some tired girl a hand. She never ran to fetch binders – others could strain under heavy loads while she flounced over the stubble, swinging her sickle like a dainty miss.

That's how they hashed over their affairs, as they smoked and relaxed of an evening.

Chapters 1 and 2 of Próbatétel (The Test), *1952.*

A Mess of Potato

'Gimme some grub', the man cried out in his sleep. 'I'm hungry! Daddy, it's the master's wife . . . even on a Sunday . . . Daddy, it's dark in here. The dogs next door – you hear them howling? A chunk of bread . . . a big slice, Dad . . .'

The door opened. In the streaming moonlight a fat old woman with flabby ankles went up to the bed in her long nightshirt, a shawl thrown over her shoulders. Searchingly, she looked at the sleeper: in the fallow moonlight his thin, pointed nose, his carefully waxed moustache-tips, showing against a white pillow, made him look even more spiky than he was by the light of day. She stooped over him and flipped his nose with her forefinger.

'It's pinching me . . .' the sleeper cried plaintively, and turned over.

The old woman burst out laughing and gave his nose another flip. The response this time was a growl, like a dog's. Touching his bared shoulder which felt sharp like an unpleasant memory, she shook it with her padded, fleshy hands. Hajduska sat up on his bed.

'What were you talking about?' asked the old woman.

Still drowsy, the man looked round in the narrow bunk. The tips of his long, grey moustache twitched nervously.

'Me?'

'Babbling in your sleep. More than we've heard you talk by day in a whole year', said his mother-in-law. 'What's the trouble? Waking up people at night – '

'What did I say?' the man asked, quite shocked, 'Did they hear it on the other side?'

Again the old woman laughed – 'Did they hear it! Your daughter asked from the other room whom they were murdering over here, she was too scared to come and see for herself.'

'Whew! Holy fetters!' the man groaned, bashfully pulling in his head between his loose shoulders. He fell silent. He watched his toes wiggle under the blanket, then resolutely twirled his moustache with both hands. 'Go back to bed', he muttered. 'I'll hold my tongue.'

'Have you got stomach-ache?' his mother-in-law repeated, her forehead creased over with curiosity. 'Or are you hungry?'

With great deliberation the man lowered first one foot, then the other onto the floor-boards, wound the blanket round his waist, and stood up. He was so lanky that it took him the length of a good yawn to straighten up. In spite of herself, the old woman drew back. His threatening, thinly twisted moustache, his pointed shoulders, the upturned toes of his feet gave him the air of one going to the attack. His glance, too, was piercing. He carried his elbows turned outwards, always on the ready, and his knees cut sternly into space at every step he took.

'What's wrong with your belly?' the old woman asked again, sidling up to the door.

Hajduska put his large, spade-like hands on his stomach.

'Nothing at all', he said.

The old woman tightened her shawl over her shoulders. 'That factory grub doesn't agree with you, son, does it now?' She winked at him. 'Say, why don't you tell the wife to cook for you? It's near on thirty years that I had the two of you marry, she should know your tummy by now.'

'There is nothing wrong with my stomach', said the man. Under his mother-in-law's whimsical glance he quickly let his hands slide from his belly.

Some three weeks ago he got food poisoning at the factory: dough had been made with ducks' eggs, and over a hundred people fell ill. Hajduska got away with a couple of days' vomiting and fasting, but his poor stomach remained the worse for it: in the moonlight his face was still furrowed with black hollows. 'You don't dare ask your wife, eh?' the old woman said with a glint in her eye, nudging towards the wall: from behind it came the woman's well-fed, contented breathing. 'You are a kind soul, bless your little heart, didn't I make a good choice for my daughter?'

'Go back to sleep, or you'll catch cold!' said the man.

He did not lie down again for fear of talking in his sleep and waking up the neighbours. From a chest in the corner he took two wooden puppets he had carved, and shoving his three-legged stool into the moonlight by the doorway, he traced nice curly hair onto their heads with a delicate file. By the time he had them ready, dawn was breaking. He tiptoed into the kitchen, lit a fire in the stove and cooked his coffee. His daughter used to get up half-an-hour later and see her husband off to the small shop round the corner where he worked. His wife would still be sleeping. She was used to it from a young girl, having been brought up by her father, a master-blacksmith at the manor, in the genteel ways that befit a craftsman's daughter.

He took the local train at the Old Buda Shipyards. It was a carriage, with even the chance of a seat. He gave it up to an old man, who gasped and panted hard behind him. No sooner was the man happily settled, than he began to breathe quite normally, as if by some miracle, he had turned twenty years younger. At the next stop there was a crush, and people were now standing on each others' toes. Hajduska, who had been straining his long neck, reading from his neighbour's morning paper, was swept along a couple of feet and came to rest between a factory fireman and a large, red-faced girl. 'Kindly take your moustache out of my mouth, Pop', said the girl after a while. The people around laughed. Hajduska looked out of the window, at the Danube's silvery mirror, which softened the sharp angles of his face with its soft morning radiance. Silence brooded on his mouth, weariness sat in his tousled, iron-grey hair; his limbs still tingled with the sleepless night. It was not unusual for him to talk in his sleep – not since his early apprenticeship. He had just left home – the estate servant's quarters on the *puszta* – for the manorial smithy, and his future father-in-law's house, and night by night sleep made his tongue run freely on the secret panic of his child's heart. The master's wife had made the little apprentice look after the children, and eventually bedded him down at night in the cow-shed. There the child by and by quietened down under the cattle's mild breathing. After that his nights passed in silence – as did, in fact, his days. And now this upset.

There was a crowd waiting for the tram at the Margit Bridge. Being well on time, he started out on foot along the sunswept Martyrs' Road. Under a doorway a small boy in rags rummaged in the rubbish bins. Hajduska kept watching him. The child took fright at his moustache and trundled off. There were but few pedestrians about, making for their several places of work. The trams, filled to capacity, rattled by in the morning sun. At the corner of Lövőház Street, the cobblestones screeched under the feet of the crowd hurrying to the factory. Sports-caps, hats, wooden lunch-boxes, attaché cases converged from three parts, the sparrows above chirruped in the trees on the pavement. Hajduska quickened his hobble.

'Hallo Feri, what's the hurry, old boy?' a man's thick voice called out as they passed by the garage of the State Trading Company. 'Why, it's not yet seven!'

'Time won't stand still', Hajduska said, walking on.

'And you're off to church meanwhile, I bet.'

The older man slapped him on the back. Hajduska cast his piercing, mock-martial glance on him. 'Got a cigarette, Comrade Balog?' he asked, twirling his moustache, as always, when he faced a delicate situation. He handed over his wage-packet, to his wife, untouched, every week. The only way for him to come by a cigarette, since he could not go without, was to have one offered to him by his colleagues. There were fourteen smokers among the workers in the shop – thus each came in once a fortnight for being touched for a smoke or two, a service which Hajduska amply repaid in terms of labour – overpaying in fact. 'Got a fag?'

'Before church, or after?'

Hajduska smiled abashed. 'What the heck, if you'll excuse me!' He let out the words over his loosely swinging Adam's apple, gabbling as he always did, when he was excited. 'Since I came up to Pest from the country, and that's some twenty years now, I've been to church once all told – and that was when my daughter was married, worse luck.'

'You've got a daughter, old man?' asked Balog astonished.

'And what a one, holy fetters!' Hajduska grunted.

That day his voice was not heard again in the workshop. The morning's conversation had drained him of a week's vocabulary and power of communication. At home he was not heard to say anything for days on end, not that anyone would have induced him to be vocal. As far as the workshop went, the only occasions on which he was inclined to intercourse were the ones that arose from a need of exchanging views on the work in hand. The few middle-aged welders who had been in the same shop with him for twenty years did not know much more of his life than the newly hired young mates. At the age of twenty-five he paraded his pitch-black, fierce moustache around the workbench just as aloof and mannerly, as he did the greying one now, in mature manhood. He had had one altercation, with an arrow-crosser foreman, during the war; he had never been late at work and never missed a work-day in twenty years. After the siege he was first to get back to the shattered, roofless workshop. He always attended the party meetings, but never spoke.

* * *

At supper time the wife put a mess of potato in front of him. Hardly perceptibly his lips tightened, but he finished the dish.

His son-in-law and daughter had gone to the cinema, his mother-in-law had gone to bed. He and the wife stayed in the kitchen. For a short while they kept looking at each other; then Hajduska rose, took leave, and went out into the garden. As at home when he was a child, he slept on a straw mattress in a small outhouse until the winter cold drove him into the house.

He felt tired. He stripped rightaway and lay down. But hardly had he fallen asleep, when once more the door was thrown open. His wife, carrying a lamp – for the lowly house at Old Buda had no electric lighting – stooped over the mattress.

'Can't you hold your tongue?' Her spectacles glinted irascibly above her slightly bloated, pallid face.

Hajduska jerked himself up on his bed. His eyes were blood-shot.

'Was I hollering again?' he grumbled.

'Plague on your tongue', the woman panted. 'This last half hour I was waiting for you to stop. What have you got against me, anyway?'

'Against you?'

The woman banged the paraffin-lamp on the table, viciously – the flame rushed to the top of the cylinder, throwing a glare over the shed, like a flash of lightning.

'What did I say?' the man asked, bending forward.

The woman said nothing.

'And didn't you know I had a game leg when you married me?' she asked, her lips white with rage.

'Holy fetters!' Hajduska grunted, 'did I get on to that?'

'You did, you did', the woman squealed, that's what you got on to – my limping foot, and you kept it up a full half-hour.'

The man turned his face away.

'Has it only just dawned on you – twenty five years after? I was good enough for you and my father's shop was good enough to marry into, wasn't it? Who forced you to marry me, anyhow? D'you think I couldn't have found anything better than your grimy journeyman's mug? I could even have found a gentleman to marry me, who would have paid me respect. What's biting you now, after twenty-five years, to speak ill of me because of my game leg?'

The man raised his eyes up to her.

'I never touched on it with a word, Mari', he said softly. Not since you are my wife could you have heard me say a word on that.'

The wind thrust open the rough door and swept dry, rustling leaves into the shed. The tinkling of a tram was heard, as it moved off along the Vörösvári Road. An instant after the boom of a ship's horn cut in from the Danube.

The woman stopped her ears with both hands.

'That's what you were hiding in that rotten soul of yours', she said, choking with rage. 'I'm hobbling, I'm a miser, I'm starving you! Starving you, if you please! And who or what gave you food poisoning? My noodles, perhaps? Or do you think the miserable two hundred forints you bring home on Fridays will feed you on sirloin steak all the week? You think I didn't notice that you pulled a face at supper? Of course, a mess of potato isn't good enough for you. And the hobbling wife isn't good enough, either. A younger one might do, eh . . .? Sirloin steak, eh . . .? I'd stuff your guts with stinky, maggoty sirloin steak!'

'Mari', the man said quietly, with an imploring look at his wife, 'I haven't said anything.'

'But you have, in your dream', the woman shrieked.

The door was still ajar. Outside stood an old walnut tree. From the neighbour's fence a slight fragrance of mock-orange came wafting in. From the street, too, the summer's stillness flooded by between the din of one tram and the next. Only the barking of dogs was needed for the stillness to trail the memory of a long low line of thatched houses, farmhands' quarters on a distant *puszta*. Out of the corner of his eye Hajduska glanced up at his wife, her wrinkled face, her sagging figure, her swollen feet. She was still every inch the master's daughter. She was used to wearing genteel clothes, such as were worn at the manor house. Even now she had a pink nightdress on that went down to the ankles.

'Mari', he said, 'you know quite well.'

The woman flashed her eyes at him. 'Know what?'

'Why I married you.'

'Why?' Her bloated face went white again.

'Because your father ordered me to', Hajduska murmured.

'Why did you let him order you about?' the woman said, in an unexpectedly small voice, drawling ironically. She clasped her hands over her nightgown and leant against the whitewashed boards of the partition. 'Why did you let him? Would he have sent the police after you?'

'Not that, he wouldn't.'

'Then why?'

Hajduska said with eyes downcast:

'Because your father would have kicked me out of the shop.'

'Did he tell you?'

'He did.'

Surprisingly, the woman burst out laughing: 'You were a rotter then, and you are a rotter now', she said.

She turned and went. Hajduska glanced after her. Under the pink nightgown she wrenched forward her game leg, which was out by the length of an inch, so violently, as if it had been screwed on and she were scared it might come undone. A limping white dog they had at home when he was a boy came to his mind at times: it had walked like that. It had been run over by a cart and used to jerk its head at every step, as if with each step it took it raised a protest against the way of the world.

Next morning Hajduska left without breakfast. His wife was a light sleeper, and he wanted to avoid waking her, as he tottered about in the kitchen. Hardly had he settled in at his work-bench in the shop, put out his tools, pushed his cap well down over his forehead and put on his work-gloves and leather apron, when he was told to go to the party office. Comrade Józsa, the party secretary, had risen from the welding shop himself. For some ten years they had been working side by side, grilling the iron. In the plant Józsa was the only one to know Hajduska's family, his wife, his daughter and son-in-law, and the only one to have got together with him every now and then outside the factory gates over a drink – which Józsa invariably stood him – or for an afternoon's angling in the shipyard backwaters.

'Here I am', Hajduska said, on the defensive, piercing the air right and left with his moustache-tips.

They were alone in the office. 'Hello', said the dark-skinned secretary. He had a gypsy face. 'Put on your cap and sit down. Still parading the crow-bar under your nose?'

Hajduska put his cap on the desk before him. He would not stay covered in a room. He even took his cap off in the privy. His face was sorely drawn after the sleepless nights. His stiff leather apron bulged out over his sunken chest.

'You are thin in the cross-cut, mate', said the secretary, sizing up the man before him with a quick, lively glance. 'Anything wrong?'

Hajduska raised his mock-martial, piercing eyes at him.

'Nothing at all.'

'I wonder.'

'Nothing', Hajduska repeated.

The secretary laughed, baring his yellow teeth.

'Do you know why I called you?'

Hajduska looked at him: 'You'll tell me.'

'What a rotter you are, Feri', the secretary said, suddenly in earnest. 'That's what you were ten years ago, and that's what you remained to this day. You do yourself no service, nor the world either, by stuffing things down under.'

Hajduska gazed at his large, blue-veined hands, sprawling on the table.

The secretary waited a little.

'Well?' he said, not unkindly.

'I'm doing my job', Hajduska snorted.

'No, you aren't' the secretary said quietly. 'You aren't doing your job merely by plodding through the day's work in the shop nor coming each week to party meetings, and never saying a word. You know quite well what I mean.'

Hajduska looked out of the window. A lorry, piled high with aluminium scrap, had stopped before the office building. Turning his head further back, he could see the gates opposite with the clocking-in board, that kept record of his life for twenty years. Beyond the lorry the upper part of the wooden stairs, leading to the apprentices' school, was visible. Three boys sat on the banisters, dangling their feet. Judging from their mouths they were whistling a tune but its sound was drowned by the roar of the engine.

'That one's my son', said the secretary, 'the one sitting to the left. He better learn the trade. And what about your end? No grandson yet?'

Hajduska stood up, abruptly.

'Why did you call me?' he asked in a flurry. 'What do you want?' The secretary beamed at him. 'No need to get ruffled', he said. 'I want you to work for the Party.'

Hajduska shook his head slowly.

'Can't be done.'

'Why?'

'Because it can't', he rapped out. 'Can I go?'

By now the secretary laughed all over his whole dark sprightly face, showing his large, yellow teeth.

'You can't! Last night you were elected shop steward to represent a group of ten', he hollered at the top of his voice, for a second lorry had driven in, and in the combined rattle of the two engines you couldn't hear your own voice. 'I told them you were a nit-wit, but they wouldn't listen', he shouted even louder, for the telephone had started ringing, 'they argued, you've been in the union since the year 'Twenty-nine, and it was time you were given a chance. Fill in that questionnaire!'

On his way back to the workshop Hajduska tripped over a protruding iron hook and fell, as he had not fallen since he was a small boy, flat on his stomach. 'Seems, you've a good few pints in you, mate', said a pattern-maker who came by and helped him up. They had a nodding acquaintance. In the shop Hajduska went straight to his bench, sixth booth from the door. Here he had worked from the time he had come to the factory. Two oxy-acetylene welders sat next to the door. One was warming his pint of milk, allotted on public health grounds with the flame from his blow-pipe. The crane hauled a transformer-case towards the other end of the long, narrow workshop. With oil drums standing in rows three deep along the free wall of the shop, he could not get past the crane. He stopped in front of one of the booths, with his back to the spattering bunch of silver-blue sparks, the pernicious light that eats into the unprotected eye, watching the crane to see where it would stop. It came to a halt before his own booth.

For three days he worked on the transformer-case. He got on slower than usual, he was absent-minded. Balog, the foreman, who happened to be standing behind him one morning, noticed with stupefaction that Hajduska was looking himself over in a hand-mirror. He was snugging the mirror inside the palm of his large, spade-shaped hand. Stretching his long neck, he slowly and carefully turned one cheek, then the other to reflect in it. Hajduska was now more taciturn than he had been even during the war years: when someone talked to him, he put a double check on his tongue, holding back in silence and wariness before he let go. The wrinkles on his forehead set, the rings under his eyes deepened.

One week after his election the party secretary summoned him to his office. Scrutinizing the man before his desk with a quick, inquisitive glance, the secretary bent over the pile of his papers again.

'Yes, please', said Hajduska.

The secretary didn't lift his head. 'You're a kind soul, aren't you, Feri?' he said without looking up, 'wouldn't break the neck of a flea?'

Hajduska did not answer.

The secretary waited for another stretch. Then he looked the man over once more with alert, glaring eyes. Abruptly he broke out laughing, the teeth glinted mockingly in his dark gypsy-face.

'Your party-worker's certificate's come through', he said. Hajduska looked in silence at the piece of cardboard lying before him, then he carefully wiped his hand on his trousers and lifted it from the table.

'Did you make a list of the men?' the secretary asked.

'I did.'

'What are you waiting for, then?' the secretary grunted. 'Go and have your lunch.'

'I'll take this along', said Hajduska, wrapping the certificate in his handkerchief and slipping in into his breast pocket with circumspection.

A while ago he had started shaving each day. At lunch break he went to sit in front of the workshop in the sun. Taking off his leather apron and leaning back against the wall, eyes closed, he bathed his hairy chest in the summer glow. Now and then it happened that he was seen with a newspaper in his hand. And at times he would stray into the hall of culture after work and putting a pair of spectacles on his small, pointed nose, look into the magazines or watch the young play ping-pong. The menacing spear-tips of his moustache softened slightly and began to flag, as if their services were no longer required in protecting him. Balog – who was keeping an eye on him since the dumb show with the mirror – noticed that the borrowed cigarette was no longer to be seen. He held out his tin cigarette-case. Hajduska shook his head. 'I have given it up.' 'Whew! Holy fetters!' Balog winked. 'There', he grinned, 'take one!' Hajduska had another look at the tin, and at the kindly old face of the tempter smiling at him out of countless wrinkles and left the room without a word.

In the afternoon, at the works conference he requested leave to speak. In the draughty, large factory hall, where the meeting was held the hubbub ceased when Hajduska's gaunt figure rose from the low foot-stool, and was set against one of the sun-flooded windows. The men, sitting on machines, anvils or work-benches craned their necks. Most of them did not know Hajduska. One young fellow went up the iron steps of the wall, others were standing on tiptoe, straining to look. The afternoon sun fell obliquely through the eight huge windows that pointed broad white sheaves of light like index fingers into the intricate, deserted multitude of iron parts and towering machinery. 'What's come over him?' Balog wondered. So complete was the silence, that the scratching of the manager's pen could be heard through the open office door.

'Esteemed colleagues', said Hajduska, 'I move that we install a pre-heating oven in the welding shop. If we work on pre-heated castings we shall economize on labour, gas or electric current. The oven could be heated with charcoal or with gas, whichever comes cheaper. That's all.' He gabbled his speech, he was excited, but his voice which, from face to face rang flat, came over full-bodied, it had shed its veils and flowed in rounded articulation from under the pointed, recalcitrant nose. It being mid-summer he had for a time got rid of his perennial cold, and his brown eyes had an impetuous glint as if the golden summer heat of the wheatfields had returned into his look. His face, his neck had got tanned in the daily sunnings, and his back was more or less straightening out.

A fortnight later the pre-heater oven was installed in the welding shop and put in operation. That day Hajduska got home later than usual. The party secretary sent word to him in the workshop, inviting him to a glass of wine. Hajduska did not accept. He walked the whole long way home. Right to the other end of Old Buda. On his way he even stopped over near the Danube stretching himself at full length on top of a boathouse, idly watching the incoming rowing-boats and their singing crews. Towards dusk a splash of rain came down and a gust of wind swept in from the river, gaily whistling its way across the little low houses of Old Buda. Hajduska, too, was whistling to himself. He strolled along the dark, dimly-lit streets with comfortable, leisurely strides; now and then he rubbed his hands in satisfaction, when no one was looking, though. He stopped short for an instant in front of the gate in the fence, glancing back, as if drawn to where the invisible factory was standing behind the darkness. Inside the house a trail of muddy footprints and raindrops running down his moustache marked his path from the door to the kitchen table.

His wife served him supper. 'You do keep people waiting!'

His mother-in-law and daughter were also sitting round the kitchen table which was covered with an oil-cloth; the one reading in a book, the other mending linen. The rain had gathered new strength, and the wind drove the downpour against the window-panes. 'If they keep you so busy in that lousy party of yours', the woman nagged at his back, 'ask them for supper next time. I haven't all that extra firewood to keep in the fire for hours on end.'

Hajduska looked down at his plate.

'What is it?' he asked.

'What else would it be?'

'Potatoes?'

The woman did not answer. Hajduska sniffed with a troubled mien.

'Spiced?' he asked, staring into his plate.

'That's it, son, a mess of potato, with prime pickles in it, just the way you like it', said his mother-in-law, peeping out from behind the heap of mending piled on the table. Her daughter said with her spectacles glinting angrily.

'Do not meddle in my affairs, Mama!'

The fat woman burst into a loud laugh. 'Heaven forbid me meddling my daughter', she said. 'I'm merely praising your kitchen to make him take to it. Eat it, son, it's good and rich, your good wife allowed the fat of two gnats to cook it with.'

Now the youngest of the women at the end of the kitchen table laughed out aloud. Hajduska looked at her and went on ladling 'If you don't like it, you can leave it', grumbled the wife. 'Go and have supper in the party.'

The old woman was shaking her head. 'For all that, if I were you, I wouldn't keep him on a mess of potato', she said. 'Likely that's what made him holler aloud two nights running the other day.'

'What, the potatoes did?' giggled the young woman.

Her mother looked at her, her hand jerking. 'What made him holler', she hissed, her face purple with rage, 'it is the filth in him he keeps quiet by day coming out in his sleep.' 'Aw, get away', the old woman kidded, 'I bet the potatoes were too rich and upset his tummy, poor dear!'

The young woman had another giggling fit. What with all the banter in the kitchen Hajduska's son-in-law also looked in, with his hat on. Hajduska put down his spoon and looked at him.

'Take your hat off', he said quietly.

The young man was dumbfounded. 'Why?' he said.

Hajduska went on eating. After another mouthful or two he put down his spoon. He dragged himself up, stepped close to his son-in-law, and with a deft movement of his forefinger flicked the hat off his head. And before anyone had time to find their wits, he turned round, grabbed his plate with both hands and tilted it over his wife's head. The white earthenware plate sat snugly on the woman's knob of hair. The mess trickled down her astonished face, into her ears, over her spectacles, got under her clothes and into her gaping mouth.

'You get me?' asked Hajduska. 'Give me some other supper, and quick! Light a fire in the range, get going.'

His face, his burning eyes, his huge hands pressed against his breast were so alarming that his daughter stifled a cry in terror. Neither did his wife bring out a sound at the sight of him. She turned in silence and hobbled to the pile of logs in the corner for kindling wood. As she squatted on her heels before the range, the plate slipped from her head and broke clanging on the tiles.

The old woman dragged herself up slowly and stepped up to the lone figure of the man. 'Good thing you found your tongue, son', she said in a loud voice and gently flopped his face with her podgy palm.

That night Hajduska slept with every muscle loosened in his body, with a sense of relief which he had not known since his far-distant childhood at home, in the servants' quarters on the *puszta*. His limbs were supple like a grasshopper's. He dreamt of his mother. They walked along a sun-flooded wheatfield, he was gathering poppies. One poppy he put behind his ear, one in his buttonhole, and one he pressed in his mother's hand. 'Where are you going, my boy', she had asked. The child pointed towards the far horizon, where the rain had started to fall, and below the rain, where the flat land ends, a mighty factory building was standing, ten storeys high, with red poppies in all its windows. You could feel the heavy warm scent of the sunlit wheat-fields mingling with the cool fragrance of the raindrops.

*   *   *

Déry in 1948 wrote a documentary portrait of a worker, entitled 'Ferenc Hajduska, electro-welder.' *His short story which appears here followed soon afterwards.*

PLEDGE

Odysseus

The cell-door opened and the guard tossed something in.

'Grab it', he said.

A sack on which a number was painted fell to the floor in front of the prisoner. B. stood up, took a deep breath and stared at the guard.

'Your stuff', said the guard. 'Put it on. They're going to shave you.'

In the sack were the clothes and shoes he had taken off seven years ago. The clothes were creased and limp, and the shoes mouldy. He smoothed out the shirt which was also mouldy. When he had dressed, the prison barber came in and shaved him.

An hour later they took him to the small office of the prison. Some eight or ten prisoners were standing around in the corridor all wearing their own clothes, but they called him in first – almost as soon as he reached the office door.

A sergeant sat at the desk, another stood beside him, and a captain paced slowly up and down the small room.

'Come 'ere', said the sergeant at the desk. 'Name?'............ 'Mother's name?'............ 'Destination?'..............

'I don't know', said B.

'What d'yer mean?' asked the sergeant. 'Don't yer know your destination?'

'No', said B. 'I don't know where they'll take me.'

The sergeant made a wry face. 'They ain't takin' yer nowhere', he said. 'You can go home to the old lady for dinner, and tonight you can have a piece in bed. Get it?'

The prisoner did not answer.

'Destination?'

'No. 17, Szilfa Street.'

'Which district in Budapest?'

'Second', said B. 'Why are they letting me out?'

'D'yer understand', growled the sergeant. 'They're letting yer out. Period! Aren't yer glad to get out of this place?'

His personal possessions were brought in from the next room, a cheap wrist-watch, a fountain pen, and a worn greenish-black wallet that had been his father's. The wallet was empty.

'Sign here', said the sergeant.

It was a receipt for the wrist watch, the pen and the wallet. 'This one too.'

This was another receipt for a hundred and forty-six forints in wages. They counted the money for him on the table.

'Put it away', said the sergeant.

B. took out his wallet and stuffed in the paper money and the change. A musty smell clung to the wallet as well. The last thing he was handed was his letter of discharge. The dotted line marked 'reason for arrest' was left blank.

He stood around in the corridor for about an hour. Then they escorted him, together with three other prisoners, to the main gate. Just before they reached the gate a sergeant came running out and stopped them. He picked out one of the four and marched him back to prison, between two guards with tommy guns. The man's newly shaven face turned a sudden yellow. His eyes became glassy.

The three went on to the gate.

'There's the tram, get going', said the guard to B. when he had searched him and returned his letter of discharge.

B. stood there, staring at the ground.

'What are you waiting for?' asked the guard.

B. was still standing, surveying the ground at his feet.

'Get the hell out', said the guard. 'What are you hanging around for?'

'I'm going', said B. 'You mean I can go?'

The sentry did not answer. B. pocketed his letter of discharge and walked through the gate. After a few steps he wanted to look back, but he checked himself and went on. He listened, but there were no steps behind him. If I make it to the tram, he thought, and no one grabs my shoulder or calls out my name from behind, then, presumably, I'm a free man. Or am I?

When he reached the tram stop, he turned suddenly: nobody was following him. He poked around in his pocket for a hand-kerchief to wipe the sweat off his forehead, but couldn't find one. He boarded the tram that came screeching along. A prison guard with a pock-marked face was getting off the second car and, in passing B. on the first car, his small piggy eyes looked him up and down. B. did not salute. The tram started.

At that moment – from that split second onward when he did not salute the guard and the tram started – just then, the world broke into sound. Much as in the cinema, when something had gone wrong with the projector and the film had been running silent for a time and, suddenly, right in the middle of a sentence or a word, the sound blasts out of the gaping mouth of the actor. Then the theatre, a deaf-mute space, in which the very public seemed deprived of its third dimension, on an instant impulse is rocked to the rafters with vibrant song, music and dialogue. All about him the colours started exploding. The tram coming from the opposite direction was yellower than any yellow B. had ever seen, and it raced by at such speed past a low, shimmering grey house, that B. thought it would never get under control again. Across the street, two horses, red as poppies, galloped in front of an empty cart. The enchantment of its rattle made the fairy clouds dance in a mackerel sky. A tiny garden, bottle-green, with two sparking glass globes and an open kitchen window undulated past. Millions of people milled about the pavements, all in civilian clothes, no two of them alike and each one lovelier than the other. Many were amazingly small, only knee-high, and some had to be carried. And the women!

Since B. felt that his eyes were swimming, he went inside the tram. The woman conductor's voice was sonorous and very tender. B. bought a ticket and sat down on the first seat at the end of the car. He shut off his senses. If they remained open, he would lose all control. At one moment he saw out of his window on the pavement opposite by the brewery gate, a man caressing the cheek of a young woman. He felt again in his trouser pocket for a handkerchief, but there just wasn't one to wipe the fresh beads of sweat from his forehead. A worker sat down on the empty seat opposite, with a half dozen bottles of beer in his open brief case.

The conductor laughed.

'Won't it be a bit too much?'

'I'm a married man, sister', said the worker. 'My wife likes to watch her old man have a few.'

The conductor laughed.

'Just watch?'

'Sure.'

'Is it dark beer?'

'Right.'

'But light beer is nicer.'

'But my wife likes dark to look at.'

Again the conductor laughed.

'Why don't you leave me a bottle?'

'Dark?'

'All right, dark.'

'What for?'

'I'd take it home for my husband.'

'What good is dark to him if he likes 'em fair?'

The conductor laughed. They came to a stop. B. got off and hailed a taxi. The taxi-driver clanked down the tin flag.

'Where to, please?' he said after a while, since his fare said nothing.

'To Buda', said B.

The taxi-driver turned and eyed his passenger.

'By which bridge?'

B. looked straight ahead. Which bridge indeed.

'You a stranger here?' asked the taxi-driver.

'By the Margit Bridge', said B.

The cab started. B. sat erect, not leaning back. The sunlit street's smell of dust and petrol, the clanging bells of the streetcars rushed through the open cab windows. The sun blazed down freely on both pavements and the shadows of the pedestrians, streaking by their feet, seemed to double the volume of traffic. The awnings of a sweet shop had orange stripes which shed russet light on a young woman who sat smoking. Further on at the corner, a small chestnut tree was budding, gathering underneath it a minute patch of lacy, exhilarating shade.

'If you could stop for some cigarettes somewhere . . .' said B. to the cab driver.

They stopped at the third door. B. looked out of the window: they were directly opposite the open door of a small shop with bundles of red radishes, mounds of green lettuce and red apples in a heap. Beside the shop was the narrow doorway of a tobacconist's.

'I'll get 'em for you', the cab driver said, turning around. 'What brand?'

B. was looking at the radishes. His hands trembled.

'Would it be Kossuths?'

'Yes', said B. 'And a box of matches.'

The taxi-driver got out. 'Don't bother', he said, 'we'll put it on the fare. One packet?'

'Yes, please', said B.

The driver returned. 'Won't you have one now? My brother-in-law was also in for two years. First thing he did was pick up some cigarettes. Smoked two Kossuths, one after the other, before he went home.'

'Can you tell?' asked B. after a while.

'Well, maybe a little', said the driver. 'My brother-in-law also had such a sick-lookin' colour. Of course, you might come from the hospital, but they don't crease your clothes like that. How long y'been in?'

'Seven years', said B.

The driver whistled. 'Political?'

'Yes', said B. 'A year and a half in the condemned cell.'

'And now they let y'out?'

'Looks like it', said B. 'Does it show a lot?'

The driver shrugged up both shoulders and let them fall again. 'Seven years!' he repeated. 'No wonder.'

B. got out of the taxi at the funicular railway station, and walked the rest of the way. He wanted to get used to moving about easily, before he met his wife. The cab-driver refused to accept a tip.

'You'll need your money, comrade', he said. 'Don't spend it on anything except your health! Get yourself some meat every day, and half a bottle of good wine. That'll put you on your feet in no time.'

'Good-bye', said B.

Sideways across the street he saw a narrow mirror in the window of a clothes shop. He stood about in front of it for a while, then he continued on his way. Since the Pasarét Road was full of people, he took a footpath up the hillside, past a tennis-court, to the Hermann Otto Road. But there was too much open space all round him here, with empty lots facing the range of hills opposite. He grew dizzy and sat down on the grass. His wife wasn't expecting him anyway, he thought, so he had time to sit on the grass for half-an-hour. Facing him was a fence, and behind it stood an apple tree in full bloom. B. looked at it for a while, then went over to the fence. The waxy, shining white flowers were so thick on the boughs that looking up from below into the snow-white dome, one could hardly see the stark blue plane of the vibrant sky. Each flower held at the centre of its large round petals a tinge of pink – a tender touch of colour for its bridal splendour. So many bees buzzed in and out of the petals, that the tree seemed to have a veil over it blowing in the wind. B. stood listening to the tree. He found two boughs through which he could look into the sky, while far away a downy cloud looked like yet another apple-tree in bloom. He gazed at the two, through the attainable to the unattainable, till he blacked out.

He had forgotten to wind his wrist watch and didn't know how much time had passed since he had left the taxi, so he turned and started for home. After a few steps, he went behind a bush and vomited; he felt relieved. After another half-hour's walk through narrow sunlit lanes that criss-crossed a hillside of fruit trees in bloom, he arrived at the house. They lived on the first floor. In the garden, to the right and left of the front door, stood two white lilac bushes. He went up the front stairs.

No one answered the bell. There was no name-plate on the door. He went downstairs to the caretaker's flat and knocked at the door.

'Good morning', he said to the woman who opened the door. She, too, looked thinner and had aged.

'Are you looking for anyone?'

'I am B.', said B. 'Is my wife still living here?'

'My God!' said the woman.

B. looked upon the floor. 'Is my wife still living here?'

'My God!' said the woman again. 'So you've come home?'

'Yes, home', said B. 'Is my wife still living here?'

The woman let go of the knob and leaned over against the doorpost. 'You've come home', she repeated. 'My God! Of course she's living here. And didn't she know that you were coming home, either? My God! Yes of course she lives here.'

'My son too?' asked B.

The woman responded. 'He's fine', she said. 'He's in fine shape, strong and healthy. Good God.' B. said nothing.

'But come right in', said the woman, her voice shaky. 'Come right in! I knew you were innocent. I knew you'd come home some day.'

'But they didn't open the door', said B. 'I rang three times.'

'Do come in', said the woman again. 'There's no one home. The other people are also away.'

B. said nothing. He looked upon the floor.

'Your wife is at work, and Gyurika is at school', said the woman. 'Won't you come in? They'll be home in the afternoon.'

'Are there others in the flat?' asked B.

'Very decent people', said the woman. 'Your wife gets along very well with them. Good God, so you did come home!'

B. said nothing.

'I've got the keys to the flat', said the woman after a while, 'perhaps you'd like to go upstairs and rest a little before your wife gets home.'

On the wall two keys were hanging on a nail. The woman took one and shut the door behind her.

'Perhaps you'd like to go upstairs and rest', she said.

B. glanced down at his feet. 'Are you coming, too?' he asked.

'Of course', said the woman, 'I'll show you in which room your wife lives.'

'In which room does she live?' asked B.

'Well, you know, the other people are four all together', said the woman. 'They have the two rooms. Your wife moved into the maid's room with Gyurika. But they share the kitchen and bathroom.'

B. did not answer.

'Shall we go on up', asked the woman, 'or would you rather wait here with us, till they come home? Just come in and stretch out on the sofa till they come home.'

'They share the kitchen and bathroom?' asked B.

'Yes, that's right, they share them', said the woman.

B. raised his head and looked right at the woman. 'Then I'm allowed to have a bath?'

'Naturally', said the woman, smiling and putting her hand on B's elbow convincingly, 'of course you can have a bath, why shouldn't you? It's your flat, isn't it, and as I said, the kitchen and bathroom are shared. I'd be glad to make up a fire for you to warm the water, since we have a little of the wood left over from the winter in the cellar, but for all I know the others keep the bathroom locked in the day-time.'

B. said nothing. He glanced down again.

'Shall we go upstairs, then, or would you rather stop in at our place?' asked the woman. 'Do come to our place, I'll be in the kitchen and won't disturb you at all. You can lie down on the sofa and maybe even have a nap.'

'Thanks', said B., 'but I'd rather go upstairs.'

* * *

The maid's room was tiny and faced northwards, as maids' rooms usually do. The window looked out on an ornamental tree and to the left you could see a dark hilltop covered with pines. The foliage in front of the window made the room seem dark green. As soon as he was alone and his breathing had quietened down, he recognized the fragrance of his wife. He sat down near the window and took a deep breath. In the tiny room there were, all told, a worn white cupboard, an iron bedstead, a table, and a chair; to get to the bed you had to push the chair out of the way. He did not lie down on the bed. He just sat and breathed. The

table was piled with many things, books, clothing, toys. There
was also a small hand-mirror. He looked into it; it showed what
the one in the shop window had shown. He put it back on the table,
facing downwards. He didn't disturb his wife's things on the table.
A child's rubber ball with red dots rested on the ash-tray. His
wife's fragrance lingered over the table too.

He had hardly sat down when the care-taker's wife came in with
a large jug of milky coffee and two thick slices of white bread. He
ate it as soon as he was alone. Soon afterwards, the ground-floor
tenant's wife rang the bell. She also brought coffee, bread and
butter, sausage and a red apple like the ones he had seen in the
small shop in the street. She put the tray on the table. His eyes
were moist and she left after a few minutes. When B. was alone,
he ate it. He still hadn't wound his wrist watch and didn't know
how long he'd been sitting near the window. The window looked
out on the back garden where there was no one. The tree had
leaves with white borders which rustled lightly in the wind, and the
afternoon light glowed on the white-washed walls of the tiny room.

When he had breathed in so much of his wife's fragrance that
he didn't notice it any more, he went down into the street near
the garden gate. Soon afterwards his wife turned the corner with
four or five little boys around her. She came towards the gate,
her steps suddenly slackening. She even stopped short for a second,
then ran towards him. B. also started running without knowing it.
As they neared each other the woman slowed up, as if uncertain,
but soon ran forward. B. recognized the long-sleeved grey woollen
pullover she was wearing, which he had bought for her in a shop
down town just before his arrest. His wife was a wonderful blend
of air and flesh, unseen and unheard of before; unique. She sur-
passed everything he had treasured about her for seven years in
prison.

When they separated from each other's arms, B. leaned against
the fence. A few paces behind his wife stood four or five little boys,
with curious, if somewhat perturbed faces. They were about six
or seven years old. There weren't five, but really only four. Leaning
against the fence, B. looked at them, one by one.

'Which one is mine?' he asked.

At this point she began to cry.

'Let's go upstairs', she said, crying.

B. put his arms round her shoulders.

'Don't cry.'

'Let's go upstairs', she said, sobbing openly.

'Don't cry', said B. 'Which one is mine?'

The woman swung open the garden gate and went running between the two lilac bushes to the house. She disappeared in the entrance. She was still as slim as when they had parted and she ran with the same long, elastic strides as once, when she was a girl she had run away from a cow, with uncontrolled fear in her legs. But when B. reached her upstairs in front of the door to the flat she had calmed down; only her girlish breasts heaved under her grey sweater. She was no longer crying, but her eyelids were still moist beneath the tears she had wiped away.

'My dearest', she whispered, 'my dearest.'

When she whispered, each word could almost be taken in one's mouth as it hung in the air.

'Let's go in', said B.

'There are other people living in the flat too now.'

'I know', said B., 'Let's go in.'

'Have you been inside yet?'

'I have', said B. 'Which is my son?'

Once inside, the woman knelt on the floor and put her head in his lap and cried. White threads glistened in her light brown hair with an alien lustre. 'My darling, I waited for you. My darling.'

B. stroked her head. 'Was it hard?'

'My darling', whispered the woman.

B. kept stroking her hair. 'Did I grow very old?'

The woman clasped his knees and drew him close. 'You are the same as when you left, for me.'

'Did I grow very old?' asked B.

'I'll love you always, as long as I live', whispered the woman.

'Do you love me?' asked B.

The woman's back trembled. She wept openly. B. took his hand from her head. 'Can you get used to me?' he asked. 'Will you ever get used to me again?'

'I've never loved anyone else', she said. 'I love you.'

'Did you wait for me?'

'I was with you every day', said the woman. 'There wasn't a day that I didn't think of you. I knew you would come back. But if you hadn't, I would have died alone. Your son was you all over again.'

'Do you love me?' asked B.

'I've never loved anyone else', she said 'I'd love you, no matter how you've changed.'

'I've changed', said B. 'I've grown old.'

The woman wept, she pressed B.'s foot close to her. B. stroked her hair again.

'Can we still have a child?' she asked.

'Perhaps', said the man, 'if you love me. Please get up.'

The woman got up.

'Shall I call him?'

'Not yet', said B. 'Let me stay a while longer with you. He's still a stranger. Did he stay in the garden?'

'I'll go downstairs to him', said the woman. 'I'll tell him to wait.'

When she returned, B. was standing at the window, with his back to the room. His back was narrow and awry. He did not turn. The woman stood in the doorway for a moment. 'I told him to pick some flowers for his father, she said, a little hoarse with emotion. The lilacs are in bloom over on the next allotment, and he should pick a big bunch for his father.'

'Do you love me?' asked B.

The woman ran up to him, clasped his shoulders and nestled in close. 'My only one', she said.

'Can you get used to me?' asked B.

'I've never loved anyone else', said the woman. I was with you night and day. Every day I talked to your son about you.'

B. turned around, he embraced the woman and looked closely at her face. In the rays of sunset that fell through the window, he saw with some relief that she, too, had aged, though she was more beautiful than the image he had recalled every day for seven years. Her eyes were closed, her mouth partly open and her hot breath touched B.'s cheeks. Thick eyelashes covered the pale skin under her moist eyes. She was meekness itself. B. kissed her eyes, then tenderly moved her away from himself.

'Love our boy, too', she said, with her eyes still closed.

'Yes', said B. 'I'll get to know him and love him.'

'He's your son!'

'And yours', said B.

The woman clung to his neck. 'I'll wash you', she said.

'Good.'

He stripped. She made the bed, laying her husband's naked body on the sheet. She brought warm water in a tin pan, soap and two towels. She folded one, dipped it in the water and put soap on it. She washed the whole body down to his feet. Twice she changed the water. B.'s hand still twitched now and then, but his face was at peace.

'Can you get used to me?' he asked.

'My darling', said the woman.

'Will you sleep with me tonight?'

'Yes', she said.

'Where does the boy sleep?'

'I'll make a bed for him on the floor', said the woman. 'He sleeps soundly.'

'Will you stay with me all night?'

'Yes', said the woman, every night as long as we live.'

* * *

Irodalmi Ujság (Literary Gazette) *of Budapest, July 28, 1956 under the title of* 'Szerelem' (Love).

Galileo

(Galileo's room in the Villa Medici. It is small, but arranged with taste and distinction. Next to the window there is a table with books and experimental apparatus. In the back a door leads out into the hall, which is brighter than the foreground. To the right a door leads to the other room of Galileo's living quarters. Galileo is seated in a large easy-chair in the middle of the room. The maid Giulietta is kneeling in front of him, wrapping up his feet. Galileo's serving-man is standing at a little distance from them. Signora Niccolini is sitting on a couch to the right, working at her embroidery. It is morning.)

GIULIETTA *(wrapping towels around Galileo's feet)*: Does it still ache? . . . Or is it better? *(She hands the servant a small bag wrapped in linen.)* Take this, and go and have a rest. I'll stay on. *(The servant goes out.)* Poor beggar, he had a long night of it. *(She also sits down on a stool and takes up her embroidery.)*

SIGNORA NICCOLINI: It looks like another hot day.

GIULIETTA: The gardener brought in a bucket of ice. As it melts, it gives off a little coolness. *(Silence.)*

GALILEO: I wonder, do you have a Plato in Greek? . . . It seems to me that we read it together, Prince Cesi and I, in 'Thirty – or was it in 'Twenty-three?

SIGNORA NICCOLINI: Do you need it?

GIULIETTA: Is it a book that's wanted? I'll go and get it from the Secretary.

GALILEO: Oh, no, no.

SIGNORA NICCOLINI: I'm sure we have it in Latin, in the Ficino edition. That is my own copy. I had it out of the Riccardi family library. Would you like me . . .

GALILEO: Oh, no, no, it was just a stray thought . . . An old man's mind is like the sea; leave it to itself, and it will throw out its mass of flotsam.

SIGNORA NICCOLINI: Unfortunately, I was able to read it only in Latin, with Father Alonso's help. The late lamented Prince Cesi tried to persuade me to learn Greek – that, he said, was the truest of joys: to read Plato in the original.

GALILEO: A great joy it is . . . It was just this that led me on . . . (*He breaks off.*)

SIGNORA NICCOLINI: (*looks at him inquiringly.*)

GALILEO: To the writing of dialogues, I mean. (*A long silence.*) See, what an old man's head is worth . . . I'm racking my brain – no use, I cannot recall it. All I get is An . . . Ancy . . . I mean the one that informed against that poor sage of the market-place, Socrates . . . you remember – for leading the youth astray . . . and not honouring the city gods.

SIGNORA NICCOLINI: Was it not Melitos?

GALILEO: Anytos it was . . . Melitos was the other one. (*Short silence.*) We, too, have our Anytoses. But no Socrates who knows how to die.

SIGNORA NICCOLINI (*busy with her embroidery*): We in this house, and many others, do not feel as you do.

GALILEO (*taking no heed of her*): We make our children read about him, as if that alone would enable them to follow in his footsteps . . . Yet virtue is a tender plant, it will take root only in a temperate climate. Under harsher skies only rage and perfidy thrive – at best a grim stubbornness. What good is virtue in Italy? To be read about in our learned academies, so long, that is, as they are not closed down.

SIGNORA NICCOLINI: We have not only read about it. We have seen it in action.

GALILEO: We extol Socrates, but even more we ought to extol his times for nurturing heroism, though even his times had their failings – Still, you remember, he spoke up in his defence in the market-place of Athens. And his disciples were allowed in his prison. He talked with them on the soul's immortality. There was no executioner to shackle him like a beast. A friendly slave brought him the hemlock, and he emptied the cup himself.

SIGNORA NICCOLINI (*getting up*): Do not allow such thoughts to torture you.

GALILEO: Man always had an insatiable urge to mangle his betters who proved to be his betters precisely by their dedication to the service of man.

SIGNORA NICCOLINI: You must not mistake the Anytoses for mankind.

GALILEO: No, the Anytoses contrive to act behind the back of mankind, lining up officialdom in front. Their ravenous savagery has been known to all who desired to attain greatness in life, but not all were deft enough to circumvent it . . . In that courtroom – not for nothing did the crucifix stare at me . . . the slumping limbs were nearly torn from the nails, poor Christ, as His body's weight dragged Him forward . . .

SIGNORA NICCOLINI: Giulietta dear, go downstairs and see that Cook prepares the artichokes the way Signor Galileo likes them. (*Giulietta goes out.*)

GALILEO: Thank you, now we are alone. I forget too easily that I must not talk of anything that happened there. Under pain of ex-communication! (*A long silence. Then, with a sudden outburst.*) Why did I do it, why? Once in Pisa, when I was still young, I went to see a heretic burnt. I was curious – to know how long it would take. It was not the flames that killed him, but the smoke. The logs were damp, he fainted immediately . . . After what they made me suffer . . .

SIGNORA NICCOLINI (*unable to resist, she covers his eyes with her hands*): You must not dwell on that.

GALILEO: Few can imagine how the ramshackle body, like an old cart that barely holds together, can still hurt when it is disjointed . . . Yet it wasn't the pain. To be at their mercy! Exposed to their glances! To the naked intent – that was the word they used: 'intent' . . . mine, theirs.

SIGNORA NICCOLINI: Their acts wrought havoc on their own selves. Pain passes, but their ignominy . . .

GALILEO: And mine? Why did I stoop to do it? Why did I gratify them by debasing myself? To go down on my knees, flanked by those burning candles, and profess under oath as my own true faith and belief what my resurrected dust on Judgment Day would only grudgingly accept from God Himself! . . . And why? Only to evade that one last measure of suffering and indignity?

SIGNORA NICCOLINI: For our dear sakes. For us, happy and proud to breathe the same air with you, Signor Galileo. And for the sake, too, of what you are still going to achieve.

GALILEO: Achieve? To disintegrate – that's all. I have undone my life's work and my personal honour by an oath. Now another executioner – the gout – may take over, to separate body from soul.

SIGNORA NICCOLINI: Signor Galileo is known to have said, and his friends also uphold, that the new book you have started to write on the motion of bodies is going to be even more important than the other, the ill-fated one.

GALILEO: Book, indeed! I am past writing books. Do not let me hear the word writing again, Signora Niccolini. (*A long silence.*) True, the Church holds that the will is free. But have you never experienced that single instant which decides, as though at a crossroads, the course our life will take ever after? . . . This was not the first time it happened to me. When I left the Republic of Venice – my home in Padua, the quiet life of old . . . One walks forth, mechanically, like a sleepwalker, in a set direction, wherever it may be . . .

SIGNORA NICCOLINI: Yes, oh yes, I know that feeling. As though you were going blindfold, and a god were leading you to go where you must.

GALILEO: In truth it depended on me alone. I could have had my revenge – forced them to burn me: You wormed out my 'intent' – very well, go one step further – be the Pope who had Galileo burnt, out of petty vengeance under pretext of Joshua and the revolving Earth. I saw alarm creep into their faces. They tried persuasion. Then I was overcome with a terrible feeling of tiredness, and as I see it clearly now, I went under in this tiredness of body and soul, and ever afterwards I drifted, carried along in a surging sea as by the strong arm of a sailor, clinging to a bare plank.

SIGNORA NICCOLINI: It was right so. On to freedom, and work!

GALILEO: Freedom – . A carriage stopped before the house a minute ago. You never noticed it, Signora Niccolini, am I right? I did, though. My eyes are going, but my ears are alert. Any minute I expect them to come and take me back there . . . Am I not a prisoner at the Holy Office's pleasure?

SIGNORA NICCOLINI: No, no . . . they wouldn't dare. Rather, they'll send you home to Arcetri. And you must pardon me for this once, if news of your departure, rather than of your arrival gladdens my heart. (*Niccolini, coming from the hall, peeps in cautiously, and waits for a nod from his wife before he enters.*)

NICCOLINI (*shaking hands*): You are a little better, I hear. The night was not so good, eh? Oh, the body, the body. It will make a nuisance of itself, when the soul has worries enough of its own.

GALILEO: It helps the soul. When the gout pinches, the conscience is quiet.

NICCOLINI: Oh, conscience! Leave it to those, Signor Galileo, who do not have enemies enough and must do their own hurting.

GALILEO: Have you news for me by any chance, Signor Niccolini? Something that in the light of this philosophy, would make me more indulgent towards myself?

NICCOLINI: You mean some new indignity? (*Exchanging a glance with his wife.*) No. I have been to the city. All people of good will despise the victors, and feel sorry for the aged martyr.

GALILEO: Merely the short-lived sympathy of those who are in the know. The world at large will only remember the victors' rejoicings.

NICCOLINI: On the Stone Bridge I ordered my carriage to stop to give a lift to Father Campanella, the papal philosopher. That oath, he says, should not disturb Galileo. Face to face with wild beasts there was no need for you to be a Brutus.

GALILEO: He spent time enough in the prison of the inquisition before he learnt this piece of wisdom.

SIGNORA NICCOLINI: Did you say on the Stone Bridge? Have you been to the other side?

NICCOLINI: Beyond the Tevere, as the song goes.

SIGNORA NICCOLINI (*with hesitation*): And the outcome? Did you see Father Riccardi?

GALILEO (*looking from one to the other*): Some new diplomatic démarche over the remains of the old Galileo?

NICCOLINI: The good Cousin is a little depressed. It is now as good as certain that His Holiness is going to remove both him and the Inquisitor of Florence from office.

GALILEO: Two more corpses on one hook.

NICCOLINI: The Reverend Father is truly a diplomat. He takes the blow with due discipline, except that it may have loosened his tongue a little.

SIGNORA NICCOLINI: I'm afraid it didn't do that to my dear husband's tongue . . .

NICCOLINI: It appears that relations are slightly strained between the two Berberinis, Pope and Cardinal.

GALILEO: Just the same as twenty years ago, before Maffeo became Urban. It's a family trait; they fight each other while doing the same thing.

NICCOLINI: The Cardinal was opposed to a trial from the start . . . (*Letting his voice drop to a whisper.*) My secretary is a smart fellow. He made friends with the Scribe of the Holy Office, and learnt that two cardinals, as well as Berberini himself, did not sign the sentence.

GALILEO: He cares well for his honour, after robbing me of mine.

NICCOLINI: Having been made aware of the Cardinal's mood, I thought it could not hurt if I went and saw him.

SIGNORA NICCOLINI: Putting to him the plea in question?

GALILEO (*his interest roused*): What plea?

NICCOLINI: That the Holy Office should designate Arcetri as Signor Galileo's abode.

GALILEO (*Passionately*): That is no plea. At most it is a reminder of their promise.

NICCOLINI: Of that promise I could, of course, have no knowledge. All that passed behind those walls remains wrapped in mystery. I could do no more than bring up the matter as a suggestion . . . (*With some hesitation*). I confess I put that suggestion forward only after repeated urgings from Signora Niccolini. Now that sentence had been passed, I personally as Ambassador accredited to the Holy See, have to exercise a certain measure of prudence in championing your cause, Signor Galileo.

SIGNORA NICCOLINI: Do not try to look as if you left your courage to serve the good cause in your wife's safekeeping.

NICCOLINI: Do not upset yourself, my dear. I said before that I had been to see the Cardinal. (*Imitating his own speech.*) 'In so far as the admission of visitors will be subject to permission by the Inquisitor of Florence, Galileo – quite apart from the consideration due to his advanced years – would find himself nowhere as completely isolated as at Arcetri.'

GALILEO: And what of the Cardinal? He may be permitted to recall what I may not recall to him.

NICCOLINI: His Eminence was very gloomy. He does not approve of matters. However, for the time being you cannot be allowed to return into the neighbourhood of Florence. Supervision would be more difficult there, and clandestine visitors might spread a wealth of seditious gossip in the city.

GALILEO (*drawing himself up, acidly*): He must have thought this up quite recently – that it falls to him to preserve the peace of mind of Florence at the price of breaking a promise given to a dying man.

NICCOLINI: I suspect there is apprehension at the Holy See of how the Grand Duke of Florence will take the news from Rome. They seem to read into my representations the picture of the young Grand Duke's frame of mind.

GALILEO: And they may fear that I will enlighten him on the methods in use with the Holy Office. Actually, by so enlightening the young Grand Duke I would only damage my own cause. Indignity, like sin, clings to the victim. You shun him, even if you are revolted by it. (*With an outburst.*) What are their plans, anyway? I cannot sponge on Your Exellency for ever.

NICCOLINI: His Eminence also stressed that Signor Galileo's stay here at the Villa Medici is quite temporary. I think he finds it awkward that whoever looks across to the Monte Pincio is reminded of their trickery.

SIGNORA NICCOLINI: But coming to the point – what *did* the Cardinal say?

NICCOLINI: As far as he is aware, the Holy See has other plans concerning Signor Galileo . . .

GALILEO: The Castel San Angelo, or the dungeon of some monastery in the Campagna, the better to seclude me from the world.

NICCOLINI:. . . and taking all circumstances of the case into consideration, the ruling circles of Tuscany will also be satisfied.

GALILEO: The circumstances of the case are, that they have given me their word of honour at the trial . . .

NICCOLINI (*warding him off with hands held high*): There was no trial, Signor Galileo. If you wish to live in peace, you must always remember that.

SIGNORA NICCOLINI: And what do you think these plans are with which we are expected to be satisfied? Obviously, you have some intimation –

NICCOLINI: I heard from Father Riccardi something to the effect that the Secretary of the Archbishop of Siena was summoned to an audience of His Holiness regarding Signor Galileo's case.

SIGNORA NICCOLINI: Can it be? To him? That wouldn't be altogether a bad thing. The Archbishop has been a pupil of Signor Galileo.

NICCOLINI: And he has remained a great admirer of his to this day. When news of the events reached Siena, he is said to have uttered the words, and several were present to witness it: 'In spite of all the ignominy perpetrated upon Galileo, the

Dialogues is a wonderful book, and Galileo is the greatest man alive.' This, however is probably no more than an invention of the Jesuit Fathers.

SIGNORA NICCOLINI: Ascanio Piccolomini referred to him in his letters in a similar vein.

NICCOLINI: However, he is much too astute after what has happened to let himself be carried away to such over-statements.

SIGNORA NICCOLINI: Why over-statements? Is it not the truth?

NICCOLINI: Come, come, Caterina – have you met *all* the great men in the world?

GALILEO: Neither arguing nor hoping is of any avail, Signora Niccolini. It does not matter in the least where I am sent. His Excellency, your husband, is right. As long as I live I shall be their prisoner. They can never forgive what they have done to me. (*Niccolini's Secretary comes from the hall. He stops short a few steps from Niccolini.*)

NICCOLINI: Have you something to report?

SECRETARY: Yes, Your Excellency. (*He does not speak. Niccolini draws closer to him.*)

SECRETARY (*in a subdued voice*): Visitors. The Father Superior Castelli is here, accompanied by a young layman.

NICCOLINI: Have they been asking for me?

SECRETARY: No. They are calling on Signor Galileo.

GALILEO (*who has been observing the scene with anxiety*): They have come to fetch me, no doubt.

SIGNORA NICCOLINI: But of course not. (*She turns towards her husband, looking at him in silence.*)

NICCOLINI: It is Father Castelli and an unknown young man.

SIGNOR NICCOLINI: Do you hear that, Signor Galileo? It's Father Castelli!

GALILEO: My good Benedetto!

NICCOLINI: But I have given an undertaking that Signor Galileo shall see no visitors.

GALILEO: And not even a friend's hand may reach across such bars.

NICCOLINI: If at least he hadn't brought along that young man! No youngster will ever keep such a visit to himself. And just at this very hour when Signor Galileo's future is at stake!

GALILEO: Quite so, Signor Niccolini. Pray, go on tutoring me how to behave in my own interest!

SIGNORA NICCOLINI (*addressing her husband*). Have you really pledged your word of honour? Then leave it to me to be the diplomat. (*To the Secretary.*) Please, give word to the Father Superior, that, unfortunately, Signor Niccolini has driven out a short while ago. (*To Niccolini.*) You mentioned this morning, you would be going to see old Princess Cesi. (*To the Secretary.*) And that Signor Galileo, in deference to the wishes of the Holy Office, cannot see visitors. Signora Niccolini, though, will be delighted to see the Father Superior.

SECRETARY: Where shall I lead the Reverend Father?

SIGNORA NICCOLINI (*pointing across the wall.*) In the *cerise* drawing room. As to the young man, you better entertain him yourself. Perhaps he would enjoy a stroll in the park.

SECRETARY: Yes, Signora.

NICCOLINI (*smiling in spite of himself*): There's high diplomacy for you! Except for the slight detail that a couple of our servants are most likely in the pay of the Holy Office. However! I will not have you say that I have less courage than my wife.

SIGNORA NICCOLINI: Granted! Now be off to the Princess, and mind you ask her when her husband's Memoirs are coming out. (*Niccolini goes.*)

GALILEO (*grasping Signora Niccolini's hand.*) Oh, the conspiracies of kindliness! I must never say that they were not bestowed on me. Could I but put out of mind a whole lifetime in which the ill-intentioned conspiracies outdistanced the others – They are better in keeping with the mood of the majority.

SIGNORA NICCOLINI (*turning back from the door.*) Do not be unkind to the broad majority, Signor Galileo. For I have never known anyone more deeply convinced than you are yourself that human nature can be perfected through reason. (*Galileo remains alone for a few minutes. He listens intently to Signora Niccolini's voice outside.*)

SIGNORA NICCOLINI: This way, please, Father Superior, to the *cerise* sitting-room. I want to tell you all about our new water-supply. (*Castelli comes in with Signora Niccolini. Galileo rises awkwardly, getting entangled in his rug and falling over it into Castelli's arms. Castelli scrutinizes him closely.*)

GALILEO: Looking for . . . the traces? (*Tears well up in his eyes.*) Many, very many things have happened.

CASTELLI (*to Signora Niccolini*): I am truly aggrieved for having put out His Excellency . . . I arrived only yesterday from Brescia. And I wanted to pay my visit as soon as possible, before . . . (*he falters.*)

GALILEO: Before the interdiction is made hard and fast. The true friend on the one hand, the correct ecclesiastic on the other: so does casuistry grow apace around the old Galileo, and sophistry make its nest in the purest of hearts.

CASTELLI: It does not feel like that to me. But I may not have a chance of visiting you in Siena for quite a long time.

GALILEO: Did you say Siena?

SIGNORA NICCOLINI (*overjoyed*): At Ascanio Piccolomini's?

CASTELLI: Why, haven't you heard yet? I expected to find everything turned upside down, in preparation for moving.

SIGNORA NICCOLINI: My husband had heard a rumour. But nothing definite.

CASTELLI: Only an hour ago I met the Commissary-General, Father Maculano at the Chancery: His Holiness arrives today from Castel Gandolfo. He was displeased to learn that Signor Galileo was still in the city.

SIGNORA NICCOLINI: But you may have to leave any minute, if that's so. Please excuse me! I must go and discuss matters with Giulietta and the cook. In the meantime, you, Signor Galileo, shall be Signora Niccolini and carry on a conversation (*she looks round*) in the *cerise* sitting-room with the Father Superior. (*She goes out.*) (*Galileo and Castelli look at each other for a while in silence.*)

GALILEO (*musing*): It's the first hopeful piece of news for more than a year. What a delightful coincidence that it was your Reverend self to bring it. (*With a faint smile.*) Dear good Ascanio Piccolomini! His letters always showed something of a disciple's enthusiasm. For all the world as if a certain humanist had addressed them to a certain great scientist. I used to glance over my shoulder to see whether it wasn't Erasmus standing near. And behold – the script has teeth in it!

CASTELLI: It's a good sign, I feel, that now you are setting out for home, Signor Galileo, your native irony makes its reappearance.

GALILEO: His magnanimity, I fear, may cost His Eminence dearly. It will bring down on him a host of new enemies. The Jesuit fathers resent anyone reading his Plutarch or his New Testament with an open mind . . . Signor Niccolini mentioned that in the Holy See intrigue was rife against Ascanio Piccolomini. He had been praising one whom the Holy Office had censured. Gossip has it, he said: – personally,

I cannot believe he was as imprudent as all that – 'Whatever they may have done to Galileo, the *Dialogues* is a wonderful book and Galileo' – you will pardon me, I am only repeating the aspersion – 'is the greatest man alive.' (*He laughs aloud.*) There's a vain old fool for you – he couldn't help repeating the story to you.

CASTELLI: Those smarts deserve so small an application of balm. Let me praise vanity if it helps you to forget, Signor Galileo.

GALILEO: Maybe it is not mere vanity, after all . . . Some dim hope, rather . . . (*pointing to himself*) not for this wreck here – it will remain a prisoner until it die – but for mankind, posterity.

CASTELLI: You, if anyone, Signor Galileo, can rest assured on that score.

GALILEO (*after a spell of silence*): I was very severely admonished not to dare breathe a word as to what had been going on there. But even if I decided to break the silence which is so hard to keep, putting my trust in your well-known discretion, you, Reverend Father, as a good Catholic who is aware of the law, might not feel inclined to listen to my tale.

CASTELLI: Frankly, it would embarrass me.

GALILEO: But even a good Catholic can imagine – the more so if he be Father Castelli – the state of mind of an aged scholar, who was trapped, as I was, merely by being incapable of bottling up the truth in his mouth – the state of mind in which he rose to his feet again, flanked by those burning candles by whose light he had sworn an oath to deny that very truth.

CASTELLI: Do not appeal to my imagination. I can see it written in your face.

GALILEO: After I was brought back here, I lay prostrate for two days, with even the windows darkened. Possibly, to keep the very rays of the sun from seeing what at first may have passed for stupor, numbness, exhaustion or the like – while later, as I was coming to, I had to give it its true name of ignominy, degradation, my undoing.

CASTELLI: None but yourself calls it that, Signor Galileo, and you only so as to make your ear a witness to the bitterness of your heart.

GALILEO: It all hinges on this – and it is not, of course, Reverend Father, within the range of your personal experience – that the soul shrinks back, helpless, apprehensive of the signs to reach it from the world, after the deed. As one that sat out an earthquake in the cellar and slinks upstairs when the tremors subside, so does my mind move, fearful of what it will encounter . . .

CASTELLI: It will find sympathetic friends, and enemies that bear the stigma of their shame.

GALILEO: Or else friends abashed, and triumphant enemies . . . What a blessing, that the body's pain revived first! For once let me extol these daggers slashing my thighs, they put a stop to introspection. Through the chinks of shooting pain I still peered out, watching those around me.

CASTELLI: You cannot have observed anything but respect.

GALILEO: Signora Niccolini, to be sure, is an erudite angel, in whose mouth compassion will ever put the word that is needed; but her husband's manner is not quite free of condescension.

CASTELLI: Signor Galileo mistakes sympathy for condescension.

GALILEO: In days gone by I used to be 'good old Galileo', now I am 'poor old Galileo', unless it's 'that old wretch, Galileo.'

CASTELLI: I am truly grieved that I could not come before . . . Yet the encouraging words of the Archbishop of Siena . . .

GALILEO: Yes, yes, of course. There is an ultimate in misfortune and degradation, and in the end it will crash through the walls of malice that surround merit. Now, that all and sundry are induced to despise me, there are some who feel driven to praise me beyond my due.

CASTELLI: The Catholic knows that for Signor Galileo it was inconceivable not to obey; the scientist, that he was not allowed to die.

GALILEO (*more hopefully*): At least, so fairness would demand . . . But even if I have felt most keenly the blow dealt to my honour, the loss that science suffered in this trial is beyond repair.

CASTELLI: I brought a young man along . . . the one I mentioned to you last Spring. He may convince you otherwise. It is a pity . . .

GALILEO (*paying no heed*): What had been our aim in life, to establish the Science of Nature in Italy, has come to an end with this trial.

CASTELLI: Far be it from me to defend this unfortunate trial. Yet science has a great many other branches which enjoy the support of the Church, and even of His Holiness. While you, Signor Galileo, were a prisoner of the Holy Office, a ship went down in Ostia; no sooner had I arrived, than Cardinal Alonso,

our treasurer, asked me, whether I might not be able to lift
it by the method worked out in Venice, and which Signor
Galileo mentions at the beginning of the *Dialogues*.

GALILEO: What difference does it make? The spirit of science,
alas, is indivisible, just as indivisible as the fear that besets men.
You cannot very well clip it in one place and let it sprout in
another like a shrub.

CASTELLI: In Brescia I met the Spanish Ambassador – I mentioned
what I had heard from you, Signor Galileo, that it might be
possible to ascertain geographical longitude by means of the
satellites of Jupiter. The Ambassador, son of a seafaring
nation, showed interest in the matter. Thus it may come
about that an Embassy will be dispatched to the Pope's
prisoner by His Most Catholic Majesty.

GALILEO (*the prospect appealing to him*): Quite so, quite so. But that
insatiable inquisitiveness, possessing high and low around
me – the unfurled sail of my youth – where is it gone?

CASTELLI: In all likelihood the great cosmic systems will not be
talked about for some time to come. Research will be all the
more intensive on questions of detail.

GALILEO: The detail, however, has no life of its own, apart from
the whole. Why else should I have used endless subterfuges to
support Copernicus by inference? Precisely because he represented the whole.

CASTELLI: Copernicus, after all, is not silenced. Kepler wrote
his books at the Emperor's Court. And should the papal
interdict reach as far as that, there are always the Protestant
countries – they are just beginning to develop a taste for science.

GALILEO: But am I not saying so myself? All that's left to us is to
rely on *them*. And who is to blame? A handful of men con-
trived to make the old-established, honoured institution of
the Church subservient to their envies. They rub their hands
because they think they have broken me. And here I am,
indeed, – old, sick, humiliated, my eyes clouding over – these
eyes that used to peer into the unruly spy-glass. (*An outburst.*)
I shall always see, even with blinded eyes the darkness that
they are themselves. That is the darkness to resist! Anyhow,
you know Inchofer. With his brush-cut of hair. He stood in
the room while I waited for the sentence. As I looked him
over, looked at his narrow, slanting temples . . . Who can
say: maybe I did it on account of him. Our miserable race of
men must not be left in the keeping of these narrow-skulls.

CASTELLI: It should not have been so difficult, though, to bring Holy Writ and science into harmony. The one draws on the book of nature, the other on the word of God. As Galileo put it in his letter to Castelli, twenty years ago.

GALILEO: Who is to know? I was thinking on these things while I was locked up, and afterwards, too. What if the Inchofers are right? What if our discoveries did ultimately imperil that which they were entrusted to preserve?

CASTELLI (*disapprovingly*): Revelation, which our moral sense knows to be true, cannot stand in contradiction to Nature, which is the work of God.

GALILEO: Certainly, this is what we should love to believe. And blessed is the man who is without doubt in this. It has been my life's work to make physics foremost among the sciences. Its great advantage is that it knows nothing, or as good as nothing; but what it knows is true knowledge. What it may yet come to contradict – this is precisely what I have learnt in the course of the trial – is not, and cannot be the scientist's responsibility. And to what science may yet attain, what it may lead to, no one can foresee.

SIGNORA NICCOLINI (*coming in*): The Archbishop's Secretary has just been here. Judging from his account I should expect not prison, but sanctuary to await Signor Galileo. Siena's men of science, and Ascanio Piccolomini himself, are eager to have him in their company.

GALILEO (*drawing himself up*): Where is that young man?

SIGNORA NICCOLINI: He has gone to hunt up a litter suitable for the journey. If he can find one, he would want to start before dawn. Will that not be too early for you?

GALILEO: I shall delight in it. I would sooner set out by moonlight. Only to be as far as I can from *those*.

SIGNORA NICCOLINI: Meanwhile I have brought you another young man, who must be tired of watching his shadow shrink in the garden. (*She makes a sign to Torricelli, who is standing in the doorway.*)

CASTELLI: This is the young Evangelista Torricelli I was telling you about.

TORRICELLI: And a Red Letter Day this is for me on which I am privileged to come face to face with the great Galileo.

GALILEO: Not a very edifying sight. Unless you were a budding sculptor and sought a model for shaping King Oedipus – eyeless, his beard thinning out on his ravaged cheeks.

TORRICELLI: All I'd like to shape at present is my own self, and I am looking to you as a model, Signor Galileo.

SIGNORA NICCOLINI (*turning to Castelli*): Come, Father Superior, let's leave them to themselves. I'll tell you all I have learnt from the Secretary. (*She goes with Castelli into the room next door.*)

GALILEO (*turning to Torricelli*): What's your name again, my boy? Evangelista . . .

TORRICELLI: Torricelli.

GALILEO: Didn't you write to me once in the Father Superior's name, when he was away from Rome?

TORRICELLI: I did. I also tried to give an account of my studies up to that time.

GALILEO: I do remember. It was a very intelligent letter. (*Laughing*). You described yourself as a member of the 'Galileist sect.' I kept wondering about that sect during the past year. I did not come across many of its members.

TORRICELLI: Yet there were not a few of us who found it hard to be living in the same city as you, Signor Galileo, and yet unable to see you. I myself got into the habit of taking walks around the Villa Medici . . . But unfortunately, Father Castelli was not in Rome at the time, and when he at last returned . . .

GALILEO: . . . I was taken away, and Torricelli and his friends, in thinking of me, had to pace beneath walls other than these.

TORRICELLI: Indeed, we pondered, time and time again, under those other walls, how many pertinent answers to our fumbling questions they were keeping from us.

GALILEO: Where the walls used to be, interdictions have sprung up. I fear I shall be unable to satisfy this thirst for knowledge, yours and your friends'. I have a shrewd idea as to the problems that would appeal these days to young scholars delighting in discussion, and engage their enthusiasm and fighting spirit.

TORRICELLI: Naturally, there are many among us whom the newest developments concerning the great cosmic systems have rendered bold rather than fearful. As for myself . . .

GALILEO (*laughing*): 'I chose fear.' Quite right, young Sir, bravado is not for scholars.

TORRICELLI: As for myself, I was impelled by other scientific qualms when I took advantage of Father Castelli's kind words and ventured here prior to your departure.

GALILEO: If your qualms were due to your tact rather than to your inquiring mind, you'd still deserve praise.

TORRICELLI: As regards those great questions, you have said the last word, Signor Galileo . . . Also, science, I think, makes its decisive advances off the beaten track, in the obscure, neglected stretches.

GALILEO (*the last remark is lost on him*): The last word, you said? . . . I greatly wonder, Signor Torricelli, which you take for my last word? What Salviati said in the *Dialogues*, or what Galileo said at the Maria sopra Minerva – under oath?

TORRICELLI (*taken aback*): Of course, I did not mean the oath . . .

GALILEO: For the time being, that is my last word.

TORRICELLI (*tormented*). Responsibility for that oath, I maintain, falls back upon those who enforced it. As I said, other problems on which I seek guidance have brought me here.

GALILEO: Signor Torricelli takes good care not to talk of the proverbial rope in the hanged man's house . . . But your assertion, I am afraid, rests on shaky foundations, even if we leave aside the doubting ring in your voice. The oath, you say, falls back upon those who enforced it. That sect of yours – is it so lenient in matters of morality?

TORRICELLI: It is not this trial, this oath, that links the Galileists to Galileo – but certain new ways of scientific inquiry, which we have come to admire in the *Saggiatore* and in the *Dialogues* . . . Father Castelli mentioned that Signor Galileo is writing a new book on moving bodies . . . May I venture to ask, will it treat also of the air . . .

GALILEO: You said, not the oath. Quite so. I can understand that it is not the oath (*with a touch of irony*) that links us. Still, you must have formed an opinion of it. You say, it was enforced. But what if it wasn't? Who is to say what went on behind those high walls while old Galileo was there? What if it was by weight of valid argument that his mind groped back to the bedrock of revealed truth? He simply became a Ptolemaist, as he said – and swore – he did.

TORRICELLI: No man who read the *Dialogues* can believe that.

GALILEO: Can he believe that Galileo forswore himself? And a Galileist at that?

TORRICELLI (*after an awkward silence*): We cannot know what happened there. It is bound to have been horrible . . . I am concerning myself with trying to apply the movements of fluids to the air . . .

GALILEO: Whatever happened – it wasn't enough for me to die of it, decrepit though I am . . . Others, younger ones, died and swore no oath . . . When I was serving the Republic of Venice, there used to live there an unfrocked Dominican, a fugitive – he came from Nola – by name of Giordano. I forget his other name, it may have been Giovanni.

TORRICELLI: Bruno.

GALILEO: That's it. Have you heard of him? Anyhow, he wrote confused books on the One and the Infinite, the kind of books these people write.

TORRICELLI: As far as I am aware, he was a Copernican.

GALILEO: He was, among others. He used to dream up different human races which lived on various stars. I met him a few times at Padua. In the end, as you know, they had him burnt. When I happened to be in Rome, in 1610, people still remembered his execution. He kept shouting from the stake: 'You are more afraid to burn me, than I am afraid to die.' (*With some irony.*) This friar, now, he truly would have been worthy to be the head of a Copernican, or, if you will, a Galilean sect. He but dimly conceived what he knew, and yet he died for it.

TORRICELLI (*with downcast eyes*): No one would expect this kind of thing from a sick old man of seventy.

GALILEO: And why not? The old should die more easily than the young. They have already achieved one thing or another. You know, surely, that Socrates was given the choice of going into exile. Do you recall what he said? Those few remaining years, lived in degradation, meant less to him than dying for the truth of his ideas. Something like that.

TORRICELLI (*embarrassed*): His case was different.

GALILEO: Why should it have been different? Ascanio Piccolomini, who is now going to give me sanctuary in his home, used to call me our persecuted Socrates . . . People, especially young people, always demanded of the great men they revered that they should die for something. Of an old man with but two or three more years to live this can be asked twenty times more gladly than of the twenty year old who may live another fifty.

TORRICELLI: Still, on the battlefield it's the twenty year olds who are first to throw away their lives.

GALILEO:. . . And not the old dodderers, tucked in heavy armour. Strength and courage, it seems, are quicker to wane than the life-force. Octogenarians will cringe before their physicians, imploring them to lengthen their lives, as might a bride in her orange blossoms – for some respectable reason, of course, like gaining time to repent of their sins, or to pay their debts, thus trying to cover up their whimperings.

TORRICELLI: But Signor Galileo's pretext is quite a different one.

GALILEO: I wonder . . . I cannot see your eyes, for in the place of mine an added argument has grown to make death desirable: but your voice tells me that future generations will think – Galileo, poor dear, going down on his knees, with a burning candle right and left, repeating the oath word by word as read out for him . . . He was mindful of his gout, his hernia, his dimming eyesight, he didn't have the strength to stand up and say: 'And yet it moves!'

TORRICELLI: No one will think that . . . Everyone knows . . .

GALILEO: But still, had I done it, wouldn't that have been a fine thing? On their way home from the burning, what noble sentiments – behind their tears, of course – would have invaded the breasts even of the Galileists . . .

TORRICELLI: The Galileists are happy that Galileo is alive and that they may learn from him.

GALILEO: Still, they are only human. If anyone accepts life's indignity he must fall under the suspicion of having done so only to be able to go on living. They know as well as others that in order to preserve life we are capable of almost anything.

TORRICELLI: A man with whom so much precious knowledge would perish cannot choose death.

GALILEO: And had I died this very night? In an old body like mine an artery might burst any time, or the heart throw up the game . . . During these dire nights I kept repeating: you were tricked by your instinct of survival. You had a feeling that there was a store of truth within you that must not be allowed to fall apart, a store which this miserable, wasting, priest-ridden people will never have strength enough to gather together again. And here I am, in spontaneous disintegration.

TORRICELLI: Providence cannot allow that.

GALILEO (*jumping up from his easy-chair*): Providence? It is not for Providence, it is for me to prove myself to this world, so prone to an indulgent smile . . . Nothing else can lessen my shame than to reveal to others what was present in me and did not allow me to die. And if not Signor Torricelli only, but the simple souls even begin to wonder, whether it was really only his gout that made him do what he did . . .

TORRICELLI (*delighted with this seemingly clinching argument*): And I am quite certain that Signor Galileo will be able to prove it.

GALILEO (*ironically*): Quite certain? (*He stops himself with an effort, looks Torricelli up and down and says, almost with a sneer*) But assuredly you have not come here, Signor Torricelli, merely to observe the state of mind no scientist ever should be found in. I hope my outburst has not shocked you.

TORRICELLI: I can well understand that under circumstances like these even your renowned serenity is bound to give way, Signor Galileo.

GALILEO: It wasn't directed against you personally, Signor Torricelli. Out of the mouth of a young man, and the more so if his politeness is still too innocent to cover up his actual thoughts, one is always tempted to hear the judgment of posterity – favourable, of course. Whereas posterity in all likelihood will consist just as much of nincompoops as our own time does, and it's hardly worth while to pay attention to its views.

TORRICELLI: I do not think that posterity will judge of you, Signor Galileo, otherwise than I do, and if it does, I dissent.

GALILEO (*with forced amiability*): All right, all right. Come, I'll show you my playthings. (*He drags himself with difficulty out of his easy-chair.*) This one I brought with me from Florence. A two-lens magnifying tube. You direct it at the infinitely minute, instead of at the infinitely distant. I showed a flea under it to the maid Giulietta. She screamed, scared of the monster.

TORRICELLI (*observes the mounting of an instrument*).

GALILEO: This I started fabricating last winter, while waiting for my trial. It is a pendulum, adapted to the measurement of time. You will have heard that the time the pendulum requires for its travel depends solely upon its length. You can alter its displacement, but its full swing will always take the same time.

TORRICELLI: Father Castelli acquainted me with this discovery of yours, Signor Galileo. To tell the truth, I would never have thought that here, in these dire circumstances, you could have concerned yourself with these matters.

GALILEO: Quite so. Well, perhaps in this respect I could give some guidance to the young. The man of science must never say 'I'm busy just now', 'I'm getting married', or 'I've got the smallpox', or even 'I've been invited to a session with the

Holy Office' . . . The scientist's calling is to submit the world to his interrogation. And if the world surrounding him happens to consist merely of his own interrogators – his gout, his executioners – very well, let him interrogate them! I often felt while I was *there* – and I hope I'm not giving away any secret – that all these trials, questionings, bargains, threats were sheer delusion, and that the one link with reality consisted in the discussions I had with my friend the Swiss Guard. He used to be an orderly to a Captain of Engineers, and he showed far more genuine interest regarding questions of physics than the learned experts of His Holiness and the whole Collegium Romanum taken together. (*He points at a glass instrument.*) This instrument I pieced together *there*. Rather, I first played about with the idea at Padua, thirty-two years ago. The glass parts are very primitive, of course, we had no proper facilities for blowing.

TORRICELLI (*observes it closely*): The water is standing at a higher level in the pipe than it is in the basin.

GALILEO: You are a keen observer. How, do you think, did it achieve that?

TORRICELLI: You must have thinned out the air above.

GALILEO: I simply rubbed the glass bulb with my hands. The air in the bulb warmed up and expanded. And when it had cooled down and contracted again . . . the water rose, taking its place.

TORRICELLI: Surely this, then, is the Galileo thermoscope?

GALILEO: Have you heard of it? When it is warm, the air stands lower in the pipe, and as it gets colder, it rises.

TORRICELLI: This may become some day an important measuring device.

GALILEO: As important as the yardstick or the clock.

TORRICELLI (*he is speaking with hesitancy*): And what is it that drives the water up? Could it be that nature actually abhors the void? This is really one of the problems, and perhaps the most important one, on which I am seeking your opinion, Signor Galileo.

GALILEO: Just a superstition . . . If the pipe were but long enough, the abhorrence would come to an end, and the water would rise no higher.

TORRICELLI (*visibly pleased*): So this is also your opinion, Signor Galileo! I had lengthy discussions on this matter with a friend of mine. My room-mate holds the old-fashioned opinion that nature will not tolerate a void. On my part, I think that there may be quite a different reason for the water to rise under the pump.

GALILEO: What reason – in your view?

TORRICELLI: The weight of the air. That's what presses the water upwards.

GALILEO (*amazed*): Who told you that, Signor Torricelli? Was it Father Castelli?

TORRICELLI: The idea is simple enough, I think.

GALILEO: Simple . . . Sure enough, it's simple . . . Except, that people had been concerning themselves with the study of physics for two thousand years, and no one thought of it before me.

TORRICELLI: It seems to me, that in the measure in which science is gathering strength, fewer of us will be inclined to look for an abhorrence in nature, or even for an attraction on her part, say, towards lovely geometrical shapes like the sphere. Once we have learnt to think in terms of forces, as you taught us, Signor Galileo such things might really occur to anyone.

GALILEO: No doubt. It might even occur to anyone that the cannon ball travels in a parabolic path. And naturally enough, a mind like Fra Cavalieri's, than whom there is no greater mathematician in Italy, might hit on it all the easier. In fact, he wrote it into his book on mirrors. The only thing is, he heard it first mentioned by me.

TORRICELLI: I do not think we need to learn these things directly from you, Signor Galileo. Scientific thinking which you have inculcated in us, may well bring forth the same fruits, even in the humbler minds.

GALILEO: Oh, these are very fine words, and what's more, most comforting ones. This being so, I need not trouble and may as well die now, seeing that what I deemed lost for ever without me, may crop up out of another man's skull.

TORRICELLI: Your experience, Signor Galileo is, of course, irreplaceable. But the fate of science no longer rests with one man's mind, be he ever so eminent. What Signor Galileo and others have set going will move on irresistibly under its own momentum.

GALILEO: Signor Torricelli would do me a great favour if he could go one step further and provide proof of this. Let us say, by demonstrating the very original thesis he just propounded.

TORRICELLI (*embarrassed*) : With water it would be a little awkward. The weight of the air, if it is what we assume it to be, would balance with a very high column of water . . .

GALILEO : Eleven meters high.

TORRICELLI : But supposing we used a heavier liquid . . .

GALILEO : What? Barley-water?

TORRICELLI : Mercury, rather.

GALILEO : Mercury?

TORRICELLI : Mercury is fourteen times heavier than water, and the weight of the air wouldn't drive it up even as high as one meter.

GALILEO (*looks at him in stupefaction*).

TORRICELLI : I do not know, of course, whether this would really be so. I had no chance to try it out.

GALILEO : And if it were so?

TORRICELLI : The behaviour of the column of mercury would then actually decide the matter.

GALILEO (*after a prolonged pause*) : Signor Torricelli, a minute ago I made a big noise . . . now I am silent as one stabbed through the heart.

TORRICELLI (*greatly embarrassed, only now noticing the deep impression his words made on Galileo*) : You must forgive me, Signor Galileo – all this is but a hypothesis . . . young scientists discussing, you understand . . . I only ventured to mention it to Signor Galileo to make clear . . .

GALILEO :. . . that you have not borrowed my idea . . . I see that, Signor Torricelli.

SIGNORA NICCOLINI (*comes into the room and turns back, talking to Castelli*) : Let's not neglect our scientists. Aren't they quiet? You rose from your chair, Signor Galileo – is there something the matter?

GALILEO : Not at all, no. I had a most enlightening conversation with Signor Torricelli.

TORRICELLI : I am only afraid I was unable to please Signor Galileo as much as I should have desired.

GALILEO : You are wrong. I hope I am the man to be pleased, Signor Torricelli. (*Turning to Castelli*). You did well, Father Superior, to bring Signor Torricelli to see me. Among the young scholars whom it has been my good fortune to meet, he was the one to convince me that physics will live on even when you and I perish.

CASTELLI : For all that, personally I should not advise leaving it to the youngsters. Let them brace themselves and lay us low in noble contest. (*To Torricelli.*) However, don't let us detain the wayfarers any longer . . . I do hope to hear from you from Siena, Signor Galileo.

GALILEO (*embracing him*): And my dear old friend will surely find some pretext or other under which His Holiness as well as his own conscience will let him slip in to see the prisoner of the Inquisition. Good-bye, Signor Torricelli. What you mentioned . . . about the mercury . . . do not leave it at that. (*Signora Niccolini conducts the visitors out of the room. Galileo remains alone. He collapses into the easy chair and buries his face in his hands. Signora Niccolini returns.*)

SIGNORA NICCOLINI (*calling back to Jacopo*): Are you bringing that chest along, Jacopo? . . . For packing your things, Signor Galileo . . . There's a hostess for you: rushing you with the packing. (*She busies herself silently with the objects on the table, dusting them, and sorting them out.*) You seem depressed, Signor Galileo. That young man, has he perhaps said something tactless? Had I but known, I should not have let him come here. His face was so reassuring.

GALILEO: Not at all. You did very well, Signora Niccolini, to let him come here. It is as I said. This young man has convinced me that science in Italy can no longer be crushed out of being in the person of one man.

SIGNORA NICCOLINI (*it seems to her that Galileo shows little enthusiasm*: It's very satisfying to know that. (*To Jacopo, who hauls in the chest.*) Put it down here! (*She begins to pack.*)

GALILEO (*speaking, while Signora Niccolini bends down over the chest*): No one shall say any more that the light of the universe resides in my head. That this head must be preserved by all means . . . (*after a brief struggle*) even by means of a false oath . . .

SIGNORA NICCOLINI: Signor Galileo . . . now you start all over again. Surely, you cannot be in doubt about what the best of your contemporaries think.

GALILEO: By now it has become quite clear to me what they must think . . . A young man's glance that holds the innocence and rigour of science and of youth – it is the centuries to come that keep their eyes on us.

SIGNORA NICCOLINI: And what did you see in that glance, Signor Galileo, or think you did?

GALILEO: I saw forbearance. That's just it, forbearance, one might almost say, forgiveness. They all look at me with that insufferable forbearance – 'decent old soul!' None will repeat, as in an experiment, the upswing and downswing of the fearful weights which in those minutes were balancing here (*he beats his chest*). But what I did, the naked fact that I, who knew best what the earth under our feet was doing, swore to the opposite, that fact every cattle-driver will understand . . .

SIGNORA NICCOLINI: He will also understand the eloquent justifications which surround that oath.

GALILEO (*bitterly*): Eloquent justifications, you say. But the slave who under the red-hot iron refused to betray his master, the prisoner who did not give away his comrades, anyone who proved steadfast, if only for once in his life, or merely imagined he might, can look down on me. And rightly so! The moral law knows not learned and ignorant, nor rich and poor. Brains or no brains – Mount Sinai gave me no separate ten commandments.

SIGNORA NICCOLINI: You did it for the same reason for which you did all things, Signor Galileo – to help advance science.

GALILEO: Yes, it was the reason for all my abject misery. I could never let go what I had grasped with my mind for the benefit of men. That's why I smuggled the truth across barriers of papal interdicts, why I slunk away from the two candles that lit up my shame, keeping securely stored in my head what I had come to regard to be mine, and irreplaceable.

SIGNORA NICCOLINI: And now?

GALILEO: Now, that I am a prisoner until I die? I shall hold on to it even more stubbornly. If until now truth has been the light of day to me, henceforth, through the mists that darken my eye, it shall be my living breath . . . Have I not given away my honour for it – my salvation, if you will?

Curtain

Act IV of Galileo. – *The play was written in 1953, performed early in 1955, banned later in the same year, performed again in 1956 and published in 1956–57.*

Part Two

ATTILA JÓZSEF

GYULA ILLYÉS

Ars Poetica

I *am* a poet. What do I care
about Poesy? It wouldn't do
if that dark-rippling river-star
soared off into the outer blue.

Time has its flow and runs its course:
Let fairy-stories' paps dry up.
I gulp the living universe
with all the foaming sky on top.

The brook is fine – to plunge right in!
Its quietude, its fields of force
crisply encounter and unite in
singular mutual discourse.

Other poets (it's their affair)
wade and wallow in filth, to say
fake things in phony metaphor.
Leave them to their mock-ecstasy –

Out of the beerhall of our time
I step, to clear thought and beyond.
I'll never hobble my free mind
to plod an idiot's servile round.

May you eat, drink, rest, and love.
Take your measure from the stars.
I'll not give in. I'll not deprave
myself for despicable powers.

No quarter – nothing will do but joy! –
lest once humiliated, flame
should light my hectic cheek, destroy
my core, and all my sap consume.

I shall not hold my flailing tongue.
To the known truth I make appeal.
My time's grave eyes uphold me, strong
in trust. The ploughman in the field

thinks of me. Caught between jerk
and jerk, the worker senses me.
Outside the movie in the dark
that shabby lad remembers me.

And when that pack of riff-raff jeers
at the measure of my verse, a throng
of armoured brothers of mine appear
to thunder out my song.

Truly! man is not grown yet . . . Still
his dream of greatness drives him on
past bounds. Nourish and guide him well,
Eros and Logos, Mother and Guardian!

1937

English version by Margaret Avison

Nobody's as Poor as a Poor Man

If God Himself turned accountant
and totalled night and day
not even He could reckon up
how much the poor must pay.

Nobody's as poor as a poor man,
who must add to winter his chills,
to summer the heats of his body,
his emptiness to the hills.

All week he works and waits
for a weekend that brings only worry,
and if Sunday could lighten his heart,
into Monday again he must hurry.

Yet the doves that live within him,
star-feathered, carolling pure,
will swell to griffons avenging
the raven-crowd's deeds on the poor.

English version by Earle Birney

Five Poor Men Speak

If there'd been a cloud in that sky
it would have flamed like cotton flouncing;
if there'd been melons in that plain
they'd have been sizzling and bouncing.
'We'd take a dip. Just rinse our shirts.
Poor men we are, all five, and thirsty.
A wash – and then we'd hustle on.
We wouldn't make a mess or trouble.'

Bellowing strides the brook's watchman,
hero of creeks, bullfrog's bullyboy,
apprentice water-troll. He says it
with clubs, this landowner's toady.
'Back from that brook, no trespassing here!
On your way, prowlers, yes you, all five,
this aint no bath-tub for you bastards!
This stream's clean, not for bums to dive in.'

' – Whoever sheep-herds the whole world's
water, turn every sheep-drop homewards!
Let pond-beetles alone be crickets
in all your damned boss's backyards.
When he sticks up a new raft of sheds
or a cow-house to show off his wealth
the thatch over his head be water
and liquid planks underfoot for his health.

Let them be frothy seas he must smoothe
with his fancy iron-toothed harrow.
Let them be lank stalks of rain he grows,
reaps, stacks, he and his boy-farrow.

May he make his money from fishes,
open an inn to cater for pike.
On his head a sou'wester; for boots –
let him pull on the holes in the dyke.

At night give him only this running
stream for a blanket, for fleas frogs afloat,
so many his sweet darling daughter
sits picking them from her petticoats.
May a dredger tear through his sleeping,
wake him greenish as pool-scum, and wet,
then wash him away with his creek-trolls,
away in a swash of his own sweat!'

English version by Earle Birney

The Plough Moves

The plough moves and the moving furrow slowly
builds up the row
like a hand writing in an open book
for all to know;
its paper the vast plain, a feathery ocean
the heavens span
from brim to brim; the writing hand one aging
hired man.

The plough – or that hand – moves, the book is filling
line upon line.
The only eyes that follow it
are mine.
It stirs me, the simple force and meaning of
this work I scan:
For the first time he ploughs there on his own,
a gnarled old man.

The plough moves steadily. Although the team
is a poor span
of mismatched cows, no mother guides her child's
first steps more carefully than
that ploughman, steering now around the wreck
of an abandoned tank –
a picture to the point. Let it stand
so, in this book.

The plough and man move on, furrow by furrow,
their steady course
unflagging, as though part of an immutable
creative force.
The black loam deepens, rising to the rim
of the blonde fallow.
Your story, Hungary, is being written
here in these furrows.

Who is that, writing, all the vast plain his book,
nameless, unknown?
I wait where he nears at the furrow's end. Let me
take this hand in my own!
But he never stops, he turns and plods on, without
any word being said,
only gestures, absorbed, towards the waiting acres,
and all that still lies ahead.

1945

English version by Margaret Avison

Ode to Bartók

'Jangling discords?' Yes! If you call it this, that has
such potency for us.
Yes, the splintering and smashing
glass flashing from earth – the lash's
crack, the curses, the saw-teeth's screeching
scrape and shriek – let the violin learn this dementia,
and the singers' voices, let them learn from these;
let there be no peace,
no stained glass, perfumed ease
under the gilt and the velvet and the gargoyles
of the concert hall, no sanctuary from turmoil
while our hearts are gutted with grief and know no peace.

'Jangling discords?' Yes! If you call it this, that has
such potency for us.
For listen! Listen! there's no denying
the soul of this people, it is undying,
it lives, hear how its voice rises, cries out:
a grinding, grating, iron on stone,
misery's milling, caught up in modulation
if only through the piano's felts and hammers
and vibrating vocal cords – a clangour
of truth, however grim;
let it be grim, if that's how it's given to man
to utter the rigours of truth,
for jangling discords alone – cacophony –
rebellion hounded, hurt,

but howling still, striving to drown
out the unholy's hellish din –
can assert
harmony!

Yes, only the shriek will do – cacophony –
not the dulcet songs however charming they be,
only the discords can dictate to fate:
Let there be harmony!
Order, but true order, lest the world perish
O, if the world is not to perish
the people must be free
to speak, majestically!

Thin, wiry, dedicated musician,
stern, true artist, true Hungarian,
(held, like so many of your generation
under disapprobation,)
was it not deep compulsion, this creating:
That from the depth where the people's soul lay waiting,
a darkened tomb
that you alone can plumb,
that out of this profound,
from the long echoing chambers down,
this mineshaft, from this narrow throat
you could send forth the piercing note
that rings to the outermost vault
of the ordained, geometric concert hall,
the rounds and ranging tiers
where remote suns are hung as chandeliers?

Who soothes my ear with saccharine strains
insults my grief. I walk
slowly, in black.
When your own mother is the dead you mourn
the funeral march should not be Offenbach.
A fatherland broken, lost, who dares to play
its dirge, its threnody,
on the calliope?
Is there hope yet for humankind?
If we still ask that question, but our minds
stall, speechless from attrition,
o, speak for us,
stern artist, true musician,

175

so that through all the struggle, failure, loss,
the point of it, the will to live,
may still survive!

We claim it as our right –
as human beings, bound for eternal night,
and adults now – to face up to it straight
since anyhow the pressure is too ponderous to evade;
if pain is nursed inside,
pressed under, it is only magnified
past bearing. Once we could? We can no longer
cover our eyes, our ears; the winds blow stronger,
to hurricane force.
We cannot hide from it now, nor hinder tomorrow's curse:
'Could you do nothing? why
were you no use?'

But *you* do not despise us, you revere
our common nature, treat us as your peer
when you lay bare all that to you is plain:
the good, the vile, the saving act, the sin –
As you respect our stature
you grant us stature.
This reaches us at last,
this is our best
solace – how different from the rest!
human – nothing fake –
this grapples with us, concedes what is at stake
and gives us, not just responsibility,
but strength with it, to withstand destiny's
ultimate stroke, to bear
even despair.

Thank you, thank you for this,
thank you for strength that can resist
even the darkest, worst.
Here at last at rock-bottom, man can stand firm.
Here, the exemplar of the few who seem
burdened for all mankind, gives utterance
to anguish, owes an intolerable duty
to say the intolerable and thus resolve it
in beauty.
This is the true response of the great soul,
art's answer to existence, making us whole
though it cost the torment of hell.

We have lived through such things –
unutterable things –
only Picasso's women with two noses
and blue, six-footed horses
can, soundless, scream
or whinny in their nightmare galloping
what we, just human creatures here, have known.
No one can understand who has not borne it.
Unutterable things – thought cannot form it,
or speech reach down so far, eternally, utterly down,
nothing but music, music like yours,
Bartók, and yours, Kodály – music can pierce
this night, your music, music expansive and fierce
with the heat from the heart of the mineshaft – music endures,
in visions of things to come
when people will sing once more – music, the song
of this people, risen, reborn,
so liberating our souls that the very walls
of the prisons and camps are torn down,
so fervent in iconoclastic prayer
for our salvation now, and here,
in sacrifice so savage, so insane
to salve us, that our wounds are stanched.
To listen and comprehend is to be exalted, entranced
with wonder, our souls are hurled
out of the shadows into a brighter world
of music, of music –

Work, work, good physician, who will not lull us to sleep,
whose healing fingers of song
touching our souls and probing deep
find what is wrong.
How blessed is this cure, how searchingly profound!
We are made whole
when the tempests of pain that batter and throng
in our mute, locked hearts,
breaking over you wholly somehow, and sweeping along
the cords of your mightier heart,
issue in song.

Szinház és Mozi (Stage and Cinema), *Oct. 14, 1955*

English version by Margaret Avison.

The Hand of Hunyadi

Choir for high and low voices: they alternate –
almost word by word – like small and large bells.

1

At home his hand caresses. How can he outwardly deliver
such shattering blows? Because his hand knows how to caress.

2

Because the power in a man's fists is formed from hands that know
best
how to give lovers pleasure and soothe infants to sleep.

3

First he protected the people at home. Then he fought foreign wars.
Thus the defended fought for him – the way brilliant leaders
and simple peasants fight – for the common lot, the one uniquely
in need of defence, the homeland – and not just one but five!

4

O liberty, he held high your shield, the hero of five homelands!
And the noble result of this: five times more a Magyar!

5

Never has a hand of warning reached from this world to greater
heights
(with the mute speech of those whose merits speak for them
instead):
The Magyar has fallen but from the battlements of a great cause,
whoever tramps him underfoot tramps on me, Hunyadi.
My statue stands a monument to triumph and to mourning too:
my likeness in bronze broods over the tomb of a nation.

6

Where is his hand? Has it turned to dust? No. It is here, labouring!
To this day his faithful hand rings all the bells at noon-time;
they boom out the joyful news (that none now understand) from
steeples
at Rome, Rouen – and Tahiti (in Hungarian too!)

And, as though signalling for fire and sudden flood, it clangs loudly,
   an alarm that peals (those who heed it will hear it) or then
(in centuries has anyone, Hungarian or not, heard it?)
   it strikes notes in nothingness for a grave march of mourning.

7

This is how the bell sounds. Perhaps for centuries to come you still
   will ring it, János, you great silent ward of Hungary!
It booms obstinately, as if coming from the depths of the sea,
   or from the depths of a soul's reproach for forgotten sins,
crying out: Enough! This idle race has done its most monstrous
                                                          deed:
   for it has pressed its own sons into the mouths of their graves!
At other times, as if coming from snow-covered fields of heaven
   (or from old Christmas Eves), the ancient hope should once again
resound and renew the intense faith we had when we, as children,
   looking at the ornate coloured covers of old school-books,
gazed on the grey-haired hero (with a trust reserved for grand-
                                                          fathers)
   and all but heard his words of command – with the grim
                                                          Brother
and the heroic Knight falling in victory – as he thunders
   from atop crumbling walls: Trust miracles! Stand fast, Magyar!

8

There have been miracles. Sudden miracles. Passing but real ones.
   Oh, you here-and-gone miracles! Pearls on the thread of time!
Oh you heroes who can set right, in one miraculous instant,
   the undone work of a day, oh you essential comets,
oh all you doctors who arrive not one second too early, you,
   who could not have come one second too late . . . Oh eternal
rescuers and accusers, the pride of a country, which humbles
   its citizens! The heart leaps and lunges in dizziness
when it looks at you . . . and when it dares to look ahead: Will
                                                          there be
   more miraculous, heroic hands? Oh, if no more come –
clang, clang the bell, János, work at it, hammer it with all your might!
   From on high disperse the gold of hope with your magic hand!
I do not believe in worn-out miracles, but in the miracle of example.

These lend power to the hand to perform undying deeds,
and for this the hand itself will never die. Work on, floating hand,
    act, you power, you pulse and heart-beat of a nation's life,
proclaim: a people is lost when it expects from anyone else –
    even from a God in heaven – to be succoured and raised.
Proclaim: a people protected by its martyrs is cowardly,
    for courageous men will never let their heroes perish.

János Hunyadi was the military saviour and popular hero of Hungarian
history. In 1456 he relieved the siege of Belgrade. To commemorate his victory
over the Turks, Pope Calixtus III, sponsor of Hunyadi's army of five nations,
ordered the bells to be tolled at noon for all time throughout Christendom. In
legend the hand of Hunyadi appears in the clouds in time of need.

The poem was published on August 11th, 1956, in *Irodalmi Ujság* (*Literary
Gazette*) of Budapest, on the 500th anniversary of Hunyadi's death.

English version by John Robert Colombo

THE COMMUNIST POETS

Debris

Draggled in spirit, human, we live on.
Yet our *selves* we salvaged, when our senses
fell to false gods, dealt only in offences,
phoney trials, lies.
Deep, deeply hidden, blind, man's natural
endowment stirs and strives in us: a cry
for truth, for love, and for integrity.
For us the true distinction's here:
backbone erect, head high
and conscience clear.

*

Can truncheons answer searching questions? Dull,
thud upon thud, fall leaden arguments,
pulping imagination, feeling, sense,
reeking, and growing ranker till they maul
the flesh, and the bare rack of bones is all
that's left. They set out food and bed as bait
and in their trap the will to act is caught.
The incessant force of fear-corroding words
cancels creation till it falls apart,
and eats away all substance, even thought,
like acids on a corpse.

*

The tree was insecure, the cave was chill,
we put aside the stone-axe and the bow . . .
we turned our faces always towards the new,
and achieved power, and reason, and much skill.
A little farther – and we will lay bare
existence's last secret formula.
Sooner or later, rocket-atom-gunned,
out into space we will have forced our way.
But who will answer for it when we find,
searching the wheels and gears, the crank and crane
of the vast contraption, that we search in vain
for lost humanity?

183

A castle was your picture? On the heights?
Today you can rejoice if you can dodge
under in any corner there, to crouch
for just the space of the worst winter nights.
But you hauled stone? carved ornaments?
A skilful, willing workman in your prime?
Work with your mind, too, from now on; creation
needs more than muscle, once a man repents.
It's wrecked? You are a man. Start new – this time
at the foundation.

*

I have no god, religion, destiny;
no dream of miracles dazes me now,
nor am I dogged and tricked now till I bow
to self-appointed fake divinities.
Butting my troubled way somehow, I feel
I'd like to do something so men could toil
away untouched by dread or fright, unbruised,
not hounded down, not crookedly accused,
so that at long last people here might be
at home, and their homeland a true *patrie* –
this little Hungary.

*

Now it's a trampled anthill, tumbled blocks,
a stellar slag, scrapheap of steel and rocks,
muddle outside, inside perplexity.
No one started or stopped or let it be.
Lunging for balance, for a human stand,
I too see no beginning and no end.
Mark this morass and learn of storms from us –
from me – for you can see that I who was
whole-souled am now a jumble, just
débris.

Irodalmi Ujság (Literary Gazette) *of Budapest, July 28th, 1956*

English version by Margaret Avison

Here on this Earth

Like a convict on bread and water, I've
only my memories keeping me alive.
The chasms and the mountains of the real
make my heart thud – too steep for me to scale.

If you could guess how hard I find it to
stumble along year after year and know,
no matter where on earth my footsteps lead,
it is the Milky Way of dreams I tread.

Did I want this? Was this the way I chose?
You be my witness, hope, you speak. Who knows
the truth better than you? You take the stand
and tell the naked truth. Was any friend

ever truer than I? Answer – did I
not share my life with you day after day?
Hunched up against a wall or a scraggy tree,
would I not call you in to rest with me?

Fate darkened for me but I chipped away
a clear piece, just a hand's size, from the sky,
and carved on it for all my nails were worth
such painted visions of a future earth . . .

You were my brother, hope. Bear witness now
how I washed earth with brightness then, and how
I shouted out: Here, where I ring my heel
on rock, I walk the mountains of the real!

I am not blind, I see the skies unrolled,
infinite vortices of burning gold,
observe the screeching of that shooting-star . . .
note where the peacock-trailing meteors flare . . .

Yet here is what will grip me at the heart,
when on the market-road the rattling cart
jigs past, and in between the wheels, his long
ears flying, faithfulness scampers along –

when the streetcars sail forth with busy clang
into the dim old streets, and they are young,
bathed by the morning sun – the sidewalk trees
flutter and flip and preen themselves like geese.

When four strings ravel up our rambling pain
in the city's outskirts, and the violin
sings gayer Saturday nights, knows how to raise
a red crest on six soot-encrusted days.

or when the earthly thunders roll and volley,
the skittle-ball careening down the alley,
to watch the old worker's prowess, gleaming tooth,
white moustache – o well-loved, triumphant youth!

You were the crowd where I belonged. To be
up in the clouds is jail for such as me.
Why am I exiled then, why living lost
in earlier days as dead as stellar dust?

Did I break faith with myself? Was I untrue?
Nobody dare say that – No. Never. No.
What you promised, and plied me with, and pressed
for years, you, world, you keep your word at last.

Let me have life. These memories make me thin
like bread and water. Give me more. I mean –
isn't it mine to ask and yours to give – ?
I am alive. Well, then, I want to *live*.

Irodalmi Ujság (Literary Gazette) *of Budapest, October 1st, 1955*

English version by Margaret Avison

When I Was a Thrush

When I was a thrush, a sparrow-hawk chased me.
I eluded him all summer; I sat on a wintry tree.
White storms came on slow wings; they encircled me,
Listening to my silence on my wintry tree.
And that is all. The dream stops there. Don't you see
I'm waiting to awaken? I
am waiting to die?

December, 1955

Irodalmi Ujság (Literary Gazette) *of Budapest, May 5th, 1956.*

English version by A. J. M. Smith

This Praise Isn't Due Me

No, this praise isn't due me,
believe me, my friend, it galls deeply
to the core when you praise my bravery . . .
Not tiger but as man living humanly,
the lair my tattered heart of agony.
I'm afraid! I'm afraid! O believe me:
I'm a man, as man I live humanly,
how could I ever be brave?
Only, I dread this more:
to fail the task that lies before;
this I fear more than the grave.

December, 1955

Irodalmi Ujság (Literary Gazette) *of Budapest, May 5th, 1956*

English version by Raymond Souster

Nightmare and Dawn

DEATH'S LIKENESS

The moment's shattered – but not the ear,
the heart in panic pants.
The minute splits, and swarms apart,
a thousand agitated ants.
In sleep I stir, my being's vague,
not sleeping, not awake;
bat wings of darkness, raspingly,
bring in the outer dark.
Silence thickens without, within,
but oil drops from the moon
drip, drip, falling, pattering
on leaves of trees that swoon;
as in a cell where water drops
tap out insanity . . .
The prisoner sees, not hears the sound,
eyes it whimperingly . . .
Cell of the world! Cell of the night!
The consciousness, in despair,
longs to break through bars that seem
likeness of death. – Out there
under the sunk, despondent sky
what shades in agony dangle high?
It is I! hanging from every tree!

RESURRECTION

Wicker-warble quickens, golden wires,
bright bird-choirs warble, on golden wires
creation's cradle swings, my waking
world rocks. It appears
I *was* asleep, deep under
three blessed hours long.
I swim as from the sea-floor up
to surface in bird-song:
wire over gold mesh, warbled, weaves
a fabric of bright sound,
till murk and muffled shapes dissolve,
till marsh is solid ground.
Gardens, streetcars, factories
step out under the sun.

Up then! perhaps the Day may yet
accept me as its own,
the world of day, the daylight world.
Can I perhaps, so soiled
with sin, go reconciled,
washed clean? With work to do
I might work with a will, renew
my bond with this skewered, askew,
battered, yet braced and valiantly
astir and straining, bound-to-be-free
old world!

Irodalmi Ujság (Literary Gazette) *of Budapest, August 6th, 1956.*

English version by Eustace Ross and Margaret Avison

Wayfaring Seaman

– From Venus's shrine to Olivet's mountainside,
what ways in my day, how many ways I've tried.
The end of all the roads:
just dust on my boots,
hoar-frost at my temples,
and the bulk of my shadow too black for the sun to dissemble.
Out of the alleys I led an army.
The heroes of my imagining shone around me.
I came with an army, and at times I was lonely,
but my ears rang with the city's jubilant night
and I sang, transformed in my own kingly light.
I too blazed up, seized history's avenging sword . . .
and over my face jetted the black-red blood,
– my comrades looked to me from prison's degrading pit.
I mounted sullen guard. Back to the bars I stood.
For the forsworn judges I stiffened in salute.
– How long, how many varied roads I've trod.
The end of all the roads:
just dried mud on my boots.
Now a new road is before me, and no
vileness can contrive to slow
my start, or turn my resolve, or keep me from going,
or cripple the wings of the song that is undying.
Though the soul ache, in such keen radiance,
its diamond core grows harder, more intense.
Brother and little sister, we talk it over. I'm ready.
I sleep badly. No matter. See, I am calm and steady.
– All the ways I have wandered to be sorted at last and surveyed.
The word is what we need, more desperately now than bread.
Blaze up, blessed hope, rekindle our souls – as you sought
it first in the alleys and every byway and port,
mate,
you who bear the tattoo on your indelibled heart.

Irodalmi Ujság (Literary Gazette) *of Budapest, May 5th, 1956.*

English version by Margaret Avison

A Rhapsody on Truth as yet Unformed

By what fancies distracted, in what day-dreams is your man's
gaze lost in space across the table, head in your hands?

What do you try to thrust out of mind, what betray
with your nervous fingers' drumming, what do you seek to say?

For the staccato words are empty, as though you
once so defiant, know not what to do.

Stand fast, there's no time now for hesitation,
eyes front – for here shall be your last true station!

– Dense rain thuds through the leaves, seeming to toll
for the great thunders I hear in my soul.

I ask of none as the wind prevails to say
why I must drive the foliage night and day

and propel the clouds. Surely at nightfall
somewhere the powers will call a final halt,

and rained woods and flowers listen with gentle
hearts in harmony with the last soaring bugle.

Stand fast, and know that you must work in silence
action alone remains, to act is your only solace.

The meek are suffering human anguish without relief.
O, fairy-tree – how autumn overtakes resplendent leaves!

Your gilded boughs are immolated, cracked, torn down
as seasons clash with the roar of birds about your moonlit crown.

Where footpaths in the briar-grove are winding overgrown
                                        with weed,
the lost princes stumble and cry out beside the horses they lead.

With lilies on their streaming banners thundering armies
                                        take the field
chopping and pocketing is their job, on their swords babes
                                        are impaled.

See, they gather up the virgin's anguish in fistfuls of
                                        wrought silver
they snap her waist across, throw her to the floor, yelling
                                        with laughter.

For seventy and seven robbers have danced, and now
                                        feast belching,
on the glass mountain's top a raven sits, rasping his claws, his
                                        beak dripping.

David no longer plays his fiddle, the moonlight congeals but
                                        shines on
and there's no greeting at star-source Fairyland for the third
                                        barefooted son.

Into the silted river now are the gilded bridges tumbling.
Broken are my reins – How then shall my foaming steeds
                                        be held in?

As for the wayfarer blowing his melodious magic reed
black storms shall overtake him ere nightfall, no fairies now to
                                        intercede.

Stalled magician, know that in vain you wrinkle your parchment
                                        brow,
in vain strew abroad those grave-grown flowers, so rank, so
                                        curse-laden now.

Where toads squat, greedy water-beetles skim the fairy-lake's
                                        surface
wordless, grinding their stubborn teeth, the silent dead know
                                        their place.

In the golden castle the treasure is bleeding. The giant shrinks
Prince Argyll turns traitor, no enchantment even in Fairy
                                        Ilona's kiss.

Fairy of love, your wings shed no gold dust from their
                                        soft lining,
you climb into bed with passers-by, your beauteous charms
                                        are for hire.

Torn is your pearly robe. Your resplendent breasts burn in their
                                        white shame
within the arch of your alabaster arms. You have lost your name.

My heart is a wild boy's, delirious, panting to discover your
                                                    secrets:
there are none, you say, nor wings – forgetting that no man
                                                    forgets.

Where are you – born of imagination, in all the myths
                                                    thrice-told?
Fairies of love where are you, numberless phantoms of my soul?

– Through my heart the swish of a golden bough, nuts of gold
coloured birds, flutterings, and singing through memory a
                                                    Golden Oriole.

Autumn attacks the fairy-tree, grieving me more than anyone.
Your boughs rise gory; my life is foundering, for fate has won.

I weep, yet these wet hands are breaking down your
                                                    magic boughs,
not one of my human dreams will I trade for a mere paper rose.

Crash go their thrones, see those stern-benevolent deities!
Trust only your hearts, poor of the earth – trust only your eyes!

Simple words we'll speak from the heart, plain words, unadorned
these we shall find in our unending search for a Truth as yet
                                                    unformed.

Rather storms boil round me, than with false peace, irresolution
betray your white brow and its brave message, wounded
                                                    revolution!

You wrench off the fairy boughs; wind scatters the paper roses,
your sons, your daughters you teach freely, daringly to raise their
                                                    voices in chorus.

We stand ready, we'll take up your songs, snatched from the mouths
                                                    of the dead.
We'll redden the roses of freedom with the dear stain of our blood.

Irodalmi Ujság (Literary Gazette) *of Budapest, August 11th, 1956.*

English version by Kenneth McRobbie

I'd Rather go Naked

Naked through all the streets I'd rather go,
let them laugh at me if it gives them fun.

Naked through all the streets I'd rather go,
or have them jail me for a crazy one.

Naked through all the streets I'd rather go,
and freeze like trees do, blackness petrified.

Naked through all the streets I'd rather go,
and die as the man who ends with suicide.

Naked through all the streets I'd rather go,
act like a poor dull fool you'd all despise.

Naked through all the streets I'd rather go,
but never dress up in a suit of lies.

Irodalmi Ujság (Literary Gazette) *of Budapest, September 8th 1956.*

English version by Raymond Souster

FERENC JUHÁSZ

The Foaling Time

With May roses on the bush breaking
and elderbush in bloom, and lilacs –
the mare would know it was her time to foal:
she'd rest more often, and hobble in her walk.

A little boy paced her gently around,
walking the flowering fields to a song;
by the time they turned homeward tired,
the moon on a hump of blue sky swung.

In her stable-pen, on soft straw,
moist with foam, she would tremble now;
while heaving heavily, watching on,
reclined the swollen-bellied cows.

And so, when even hay-ricks dozed,
and the Seven Stars aimed south –
she foaled her young. Then long she licked
him on the wet-shut eyes and mouth.

The newcomer slumbered at his mother's side,
lay like plucked down of pillow-stuff;
straw was never spread so fine,
nor sleeping snow, or milk, so soft.

In a red cap the bright dawn came up.
Gave a hello and went for a sprint;
the colt got up on its lean knobby legs
and tottered, like water wavering.

And as the morning stuck its blue nose
in at the window, giving a whiff,
the young one nudged at his mother's side
and sought the milk with wet-soft mouth.

The leaves made stir by fits and starts,
and cheerful chickens scraped for chaff,
while up above, for envy wilting,
the golden petalled stars dropped off.

From the volume Szárnyas csikó (The Winged Colt). *1949.*

English version by Louis Dudek

Song of the Tractor

Kneel down, all you meek little horses,
today the co-operative got a new tractor,
a green-painted, thirty-horsepower
rubber-wheeled motor-tractor.

On Sunday the men still hung around it,
with smiling eyes admiring it.
They stroked it, tried out its iron saddle,
and fooled with the steering wheel.

Monday it was ploughing merrily.
It pulled four ploughs all at once;
it exhaled water from its shining nose
and back-fired smoke-rings.

Kneel down all you meek little horses,
all you foals with a star on your forehead.
This tractor is a colt of fire and iron;
Petrol he feeds on, and oil.

Look, we are ploughing the downy earth;
above us a skylark sings;
clouds race in the blue wind,
and our hearts sing for happiness.

Now it is noon: we are resting, the tractor and I.
A blue flower bends down to my forehead.
A spotted heifer comes from the meadow –
she smells me, and stops beside me.

From the volume Szárnyas csikó (The Winged Colt). *1949.*

English version by A. J. M. Smith

Your Ribbed, Peasant Hand

On the books your small hand lies,
as pen, pencil, scrape on card –
a small, ribbed, peasant hand,
freckled, ink-stained, scarred.

On the wrinkles, on skin and veins,
the light-arrows repose;
to a hundred twittering minds,
from this, the wonder flows.

I see how the chalk on the board
flits in your swallow-like finger,
where a thought, like the morning, shines;

and how each intellect grows
to form – like a sculpted stone –
in work, thought, for the coming times.

From the volume Óda a repüléshez (Ode to Flying). *1953.*

English version by Louis Dudek

Farm, at Dark, on the Great Plain

Tingling,
sparkling,
smouldering,
over the mute earth the loosed night falls.

Glass-petalled flowers, leaves of thin glass
are incandescent, as
our anguish.

Peculiar weeds, lush and fine-spun
dream on,
half in the dark secreted
their torsos reaching up into the void
like the brooding undergrowth at the bottom of the soul.
Suffering and sin flare up in every blade.
The parts are not the whole.
In the lucid earth-dark all is corruptible.

Agleam is all
that juts up out of the gloaming:
roofslant, poplar,
lip of the trough,

moon-tilted swallow soaring, homing
flittering,
the hay-rick's ripe-gold keening.
Among the stubble pheasants move and rustle,
the young deer nibble.
They shy away from the hare's wide-open eyes
and veer out of the light.

The moonlight's liquid glass
wells over the earth
and quells the very silence in its clasp
to crystal blocks,
glass turrets,
tinkling vine-stems.
Still – how this silence (silvery bushes,
half-guessed-at-stalks, dim files of foliage)
entangles and engulfs the din of empty space
and murmurous flower-scent from the garden-beds.

The house squats
hunched like a scarab, lest
the Milky Way reach down its scaly talons.

The sap in the bean-vines slowly
pulses and throbs
and the withery pods down in the dark recover
a new-born firmness. They discover life only
in building it, never knowing their lot.
Minerals, crystals, water,
the flesh-filling cucumber
drinks in, swelling its small rhinoceros-hide.

While sap, (like mother's-blood to a darkling
embryo), seeps through the cells,
whole solar systems circle
within, galaxies countless, crackling
as they plummet and weave:
so, breathless, matter lives.

All things are incandescent with their light of being:
the moon . . . the moon dwells on its waning;
the breathing tree on how its leaves must fall;
the melon feels its juices sweetening up;
autumn's vinegar-steam the tomatoes ponder;

the corn senses its kernels' thrust from the cob –
they have started already to form
like pearls in an infant's gum –
standing mindless and mild the horses sleep
or dream of trailing down again for water
and the whinnying gallop after.

The sow breathes heavily, deep in her slumber.
Against her belly piglets scramble
and swarm
like a moving pulp of warm
craving, a rosy greediness.
The cabbage-stalks harden and ridge.

Under uprights and open thatch
lie cartwheels, boards, scrap-iron, trash.
The spiderwebs' gauze-cities swing and dangle.
On the warm dungheap the ducks snuggle
and its breath flutters the nettle's candlewick
and nearby wheat and rosemary-spikes flicker.

Stubble, corn, hempfields stretch out all around
far off, where darkness is intense as sound.
The moon shepherds the flocks.
And to the listening field-mouse an assured bull-frog croaks.

I lie in the drenched grass.
Spice-perfumes and my senses here converse.
These flower-cups are metal-froth let cool.
The ground-flow of air stirs
and wafts warmth to me from the stubble-fields,
and honey-smell –
commingled
yet distinct fragrances.
Strange, blissful night, primal, voluptuous –
random – with nothing of passion's single-mindedness.
Plant cannot guess – nor planet – the knowledge a human bears.

Even a man knows little, has but dimly understood
how marble is one substance with milk of dandelion
and prismed insects' eyes
and blood.
Yet, as a man I am removed,
set apart from dews
or Pleiades.

201

In me alone is the tumult of human cares, and of love –
my pain, my power, are from these.

From the old earth-soaked dark – silence's floor
writhing with stems and storm of sap – to the clear
lift of the upper silences, one free, unbridled power
of teeming: the exploding star
fusing in a primeval shower
of metal-mist, condensed, compounded. Ore
vomited to the crucible where
blast-furnace slag floods off, the slower
seminal globules, crystallizing, or
vegetation's jelly and mulch, its queer
seeds, like the winking elements in the core
of the fissured rock, all crushed in pluvial fire,
molten to become matter, all afire
to become real, till the quarries
of chlorophylled purpose mire
and melt in a plastic flow
and the foam of glossy light
crams to anthracite.
With ululating, jungle-roar,
tremors of flaring fear,
in mawling, ravening desire,
rivered with sweat . . . the everlasting flood
seethes and simmers on, in solitude.

I love you. You can be aware of it –
after all, something new,
different from the love helpless matter feels,
with its heedlessness of tomorrow.
No falling star can hear when my heart calls.
The man is sleeping in his corner, the hiss
of his breath catching at a rheumatic crick.
In the kitchen the flickering oil-lamp plays
over the woman as she leans
dozing against the wall.
Her old knuckles and veins
under the lamplight show a yellow glaze.
They are both making ready to die alone,
for this too must be done.

The splayed furniture strains for a voice remote past time.
Sap rises in its dreams.

Leaves sigh, ring wells on ring within.
Whining in sleep, it is washed once more by a forest moon.

A *kapca** by the bed,
beside one lumpy boot.
On the wall a picture from an old paper
pinned flat.
A derelict watch-chain on another hook.
A book mourning, unread.

By now I know for sure what I half-glimpsed before:
how senseless your life would be, all by yourself, alone,
and how it would be for me too, a desolate rolling-stone –
sadness and brute desire.
For animals do not need
to be one till they rot.
They feed, suckle their young, kill, make water, mate,
physical to the hilt.
And when star melts into star, and all the heavens move
the foaming metals flash, and spin, and fade,
the molten passions lapse, dissolve,
all by themselves.
Mollusc and vermin couple just to breed.

Only with you I believe, I feel at one,
nor need my heart at last go so mercilessly alone
to its corruption.

Flower and plant filaments slowly to new
forms glimmer.
The earth bears fruit in an unwitting flow.
Thatch, poplar, cornstalks shimmer.
And I look on as it topples almost in my face,
scaly-bellied, soft, and huge-as-earth,
hiding its reptile head among ancient galaxies,
its tail dangling over in some other night of space,
the jewelled, gelatinous Milky Way, its girth
brushing against the lamenting corn-silk
and the world's bulk.

From the volume A virágok hatalma (The Might of the Flowers), *1955.*

English version by Margaret Avison

* a *kapca* is a strip of cloth, wound round the foot, instead of a sock.

At Twenty-six

Twenty-six years are few enough to force me, terrified,
to shriek aloud: 'Frost is tinfoil in my skull of bone!'
Yet was I given to loving, cursing, burying whatever had died
    – and not for myself alone.

Fate, destiny or something will yet give me time
– and enough strength also to my faith –
that what pains only myself I may cry aloud in a rhyme
    before my death.

My flowers are still wet with dew. By sickness my life's
    not corroded.
In my fields strut peacocks, bulls stand, foam-lathered
    colts start.
I stand firm. Flaming galaxies are exploded
    by a kiss – in my heart.

Soon maybe my flowers will shrivel to straw. Hailstone,
brimstone, will shatter my green shoots, my green place.
But, ah, till then let me flame and thunder on
    – a golden stallion of Space.

How soon? Who knows? What do I care?
I am alive – an exploding resplendent world.
And if I collide with another star
    out of its orbit it's hurled.

Who else could make men believe
what only I know
and which if the heart but dimly conceive,
    horror-struck, it begins to glow?

Do not fear for me. I am resolute and immutable.
If this be a virtue, it is mine then.
Upsurges from my lips the ineffable
    quality of man.

From the volume A virágok hatalma (The Might of the Flowers), *1955.*

English version by A. J. M. Smith

Man Imposes his Pattern upon a Dream

The torrid land is suffering,
man's awareness is beginning.
Duckweed shrivels in the fever.
All that was is gone for ever.

Voracious instincts now dwindle.
Only veined cellophanes rustle.
On its ribbed stalk like a green bat
the pumpkin leaf flutters its rag.

Also within into a glassy mess
fused by the fire of consciousness
is that which sprang up once as dense
as weed from depths of existence.

But nurtured hope learns to aspire
as corn grows on the atom's fire.
Sober hormones nurse the hope,
its cause is mine, I'll not give up.

When all's said, man decides alone,
silence gives laws that are its own.
So much more than mere beast is man,
he'll grasp what frees him when he can.

The male locust makes charnel love,
losing life, hands on enough.
Needle-sewn double rowed the jawed
teeth rip at organs, the assured

female is devouring male
her mouth's saws criss-cross and impale,
spiked bow bent in triangle head,
and the heart victim of acid.

Now this is how I stand to you,
giving all, making you fruitful
by consciousness – yet gobbled up
by you, my man-eating epoch!

Hot blood clots by the sun are made
where the tree slops its coolless shade,
the fresh green of tender parsley
casts a russet lacework near me.

The fledgling geese peck in the yard,
fat, shiny, yellow lumps of lard,
skin gritty with feather pimples,
their grease breeding volcanic moles.

A knife glints over them, concern
is poised above me in my turn.
My throat cannot be slit by pain,
I grow, transcend, render it tame.

Shrivelled Evanescence cowers,
mourning for its old psalter serves,
on a wrought brass crucifix its
finger like a green lizard sits.

My small daughter runs to and fro
pleased with her dotted ball, it's blue.
Yet her small soul carries within
outlines of the human pattern.

The strange words, sweet sounds she lets fall
shape desires so clear to all.
She plays, cries, grows, laughs, climbs
under the steel girders of time.

So might our age be remade to
this human pattern – once rescued.
Already, as life's embryo has come
the blind, hermaphrodite atom.

In a deck-chair my mother's sleeping,
on the lawn breathes her pair of wings.
She thinks up for us in her turn
dreams made to a human pattern.

Studded are her gnarled feet with sores
that flowered on stone laundry floors,
dream-roots bearing the tree of sighs
and pain-budded boughs implore the skies.

The slate roof swelters up aloft
and the metal-crested eaves-trough.
Green walnut coolness on my body,
summer's sulphur blaze choking me.

One blood-bellied yellow instant
is the poison-calixed Sabbath.
Wine and sodawater stand upon
my table. I take no absolution.

From the volume A virágok hatalma (The Might of the Flowers), *1955.*

English version by Kenneth McRobbie

The Boy Changed into a Stag Cries out at the Gate of Secrets

Her own son the mother called
from afar crying,
her own son the mother called
from afar crying,
she went before the house, from there calling
her hair's full knot she loosed,
with it the dusk wove a dense quivering
veil, a precious cloak down to her ankles,
wove a stiff mantle, heavy-flaring,
a flag for the wind with ten black tassels
a shroud, the fire-stabbed, blood-tainted dusk.
Her fingers she twined in the sharp tendrilled
stars, her face the moon's foam coated
and on her own son she called shrilly
as once she called him, a small child,
she went before the house and talked to the wind,
with song birds spoke, sending swiftly
words after the wild pairing geese
to the shivering bullrushes,
to the potato-flower so silvery,
to the clench-balled bulls, rooted so firmly,
to the well-shading fragrant sumach tree,

207

she spoke to the fish leaping at play,
to the mauve oil-rings afloat fleetingly:
        You birds and boughs, hear me
listen as I cry out,
        and listen, you fishes, you flowers
listen for I speak to be heard,
        listen you glands of expanding soils
        you vibrant fins, astral-seeding parachutes,
decelerate, you humming motors of the saps
in the depth of the atom, screw down the whining taps.
        All metal-pelvised virgins, sheep alive under cotton
listen as I cry out,
for I'm crying out to my son!

Her own son the mother called
her cry ascending in a spiral,
within the gyre of the universe it rose
Her limbs flashing in the light rays
like the back of a fish all slippery scaled,
or a roadside boil of salt or crystal.
Her own son the mother called:
Come back, my own son, come back
    I call you, your own mother!
Come back, my own son, come back
    I call you, your mild harbour,
come back, my own son, come back
    I call you, your cool fountain,
come back, my own son, come back
    I call you, your memory's teat,
come back, my own son, come back
    I call you, your withered tent,
come back, my own son, come back
    I call you, your almost sightless lamp.

Come back, my own son, for I'm blind in this world of
                                        sharp objects
within yellow-green bruises my eyes are sinking,
                                    my brow contracts,
my thighs – my barked shins
from all sides things rush at me like crazed wethers,
the gate, the post, the chair try their horns on me
doors slam upon me like drunken brawlers,
the perverse electricity shoots its current at me

my flaking skin seeps blood – a bird's beak cracked with a stone,
    scissors swim out of reach like spider crabs, all metal
the matches are sparrows' feet, the pail swings back at me with
                                    its handle,
come back, my own son, come back
my legs no longer carry me like the young hind,
    vivid tumors pout on my feet
    gnarled tubers penetrate my purpling thighs,
on my toes grow bony structures,
    the fingers on my hands stiffen, already the shelly flesh
scales off like slate from aging geologic formations,
    every limb has served its time and sickens
come back, my own son, come back,
    for I am no more as I was,
    I am gaunt with inner visions
    which flare from the stiffening hoary organs
    as on winter mornings an old cock's crowing
rings from a fence of shirts, hanging hard-frozen,
I call you, your own mother,
come back, my own son, come back,
to the unmanageable things bring a new order,
discipline the estranged objects, tame the knife,
    domesticate the comb,
for I am now but two gritty green eyes
glassy and weightless like the *libellula*
whose winged nape and dragon jaws, you know it well
    my son, hold so delicately
two crystal apples in his green-lit skull,
I am two staring eyes without a face
seeing all, now one with unearthly beings.
Come back, my own son, come back,
    with your fresh breath, set all to rights again.

        In the far forest, the lad heard
        at once, he jerked up his head
        with his wide nostrils testing
        the air, soft dewlaps pulsing
        with veined ears pricked, harkening
        alertly to those tones sobbing
        as to a hunter's slimy tread,
        or hot wisps curling from the bed
        of young forest fires, when smoky
        high woods start to whimper bluely.

He turned his head, no need to tell
him, this was the voice he knew so well,
now by an agony he's seized
fleece on his buttocks he perceives,
in his lean legs sees the proof
of strange marks left by each cleft hoof,
where lilies shine in forest pools
sees his low, hairy-pursed buck-balls.
He pushes his way down to the lake
breasting the brittle willow brake
rump slicked with foam, at each bound
he slops white froth on the hot ground,
his four black hooves tear out a path
through wild flowers wounded to death,
stamp a lizard into the mould
neck swollen, tail snapped, growing cold
and when he reached the lake at last
into its moonlit surface glanced:
it holds the moon, beeches shaking
and back at him a stag staring.
Only now thick hair does he see
covering all his slender body
hair over knees, thighs, the transverse
tasselled lips of his male purse,
his long skull had sprouted antlers
into bone leaves their bone boughs burst,
his face is furry to the chin
his nostrils are slit and slant in.
Against trees his great antlers knock
veins knot in ropes along his neck,
madly he strains, prancing he tries
vainly to raise an answering cry,
only a stag's voice bells within
the new throat of this mother's son,
he drops a son's tears, paws the brink
to banish that lake-monster, sink
it down into the vortex sucking
fluid dark, where scintillating
little fish flash their flowery fins,
minute, bubble-eyed diamonds.
The ripples subside at last in the gloom,
but a stag still stands in the foam of that
    moon.

Now in his turn the lad cried back
    stretching up his belling neck,
now in his turn the lad called back
    through a stag's throat, through the fog calling:
Mother, my mother
I cannot go back,
mother, my mother
you must not lure me,
mother, my mother
my dear breeding nurse,
mother, my mother
sweet frothy fountain,
safe arms that held me
whose heavy breasts fed me
my tent, shelter from frosts,
mother, my mother
seek not my coming,
mother, my mother
my frail silken stalk,
mother, my mother
bird with teeth of gold,
mother, my mother,
you must not lure me!
If I should come home
my horns would drag you
from horn to sharp horn
I'd toss your body,
if I should come home
down I would roll you,
tread your loose veiny
breasts, mangled by hooves,
I'd stab with unsheathed
horns, maul with my teeth
tread in your womb, even.
If I should come home
mother, my mother
I'd spill out your lungs
for blue flies buzzing round,
and the stars would stare down
into your flower-organs,
which once did hold me
with warmth of summer suns
in shiny peace encased

where warmth never ceased,
as once cattle breathed
gently to warm Jesus.
Mother, my mother
do not summon me,
death would strike you down
in my shape's coming
if this son drew near.
Each branch of my antlers
is a gold filament,
each prong of my antlers
a winged candlestick,
each tine of my antlers
a catafalque candle,
each leaf of my antlers
a gold-laced altar.
Dead surely you'd fall
if you saw my grey antlers
soar into the sky
like the All Soul's Eve
candle-lit graveyard,
my head a stone tree
leafed with growing flame.
Mother, my mother
if I came near you
I would soon singe you
like straw, I would scorch
you to greasy black clay,
you'd flare like a torch
for I would roast you
to charred shreds of flesh.
Mother, my mother
do not summon me
for if I came home
I would devour you,
for if I came home
your bed I would ravage,
the flower garden
with my thousand-pronged
horn would I savage,
I'd chew through the trees
in the stag-torn groves,
drink dry the one well

in a single gulp,
if I should return
I'd fire your cottage,
and then I would run
to the old graveyard,
with my pointed soft
nose, with all four hooves
I'd root up my father,
with my teeth wrench off
his cracked coffin lid
and snuff his bones over!
Mother, my mother
do not lure me,
I cannot go back,
for if I came home
I'd bring your death surely.

In a stag's voice the lad cried
and in these words his mother answered him:
    Come back, my own son, come back
I call you, your mother.
    Come back, my own son, come back
I'll cook you brown broth, and you'll slice onion-rings in it
they'll crunch between your teeth, like quartz splintering in
                        a giant's jaws,
I'll give you warm milk in a clean jug,
from my last keg trickle wine into heron-necked bottles
and I know how to knead the bread with my rocky fists, I know
                      how you like it,
bread for baking soft-bellied buns for you, sweet bread for
                    the feasts.
    Come back, my own son, come back,
from the live breasts of screeching geese for your eiderdown
                    I plucked feathers,
weeping I plucked my weeping geese, the spots stripped of
                  feathers turning
    a fierce white on their breasts, like the mouths of the dying,
I shook up your pallet in the clear sunlight, made it fresh
                  for your rest,
the yard has been swept, the table is laid – for your coming.

    Mother, my mother
        for me there's no homecoming,

do not lay out for me twisted white bread
        or sweet goat's milk in my flowered mug foaming,
and do not prepare for me a soft bed,
        for their feathers ravage not the breasts of the geese,
spill your wine rather, upon my father's grave let it soak in,
        the sweet onions bind into a garland,
fry up for the little ones that froth-bellying dough.
        The warm milk would turn to vinegar at my
                                    tongue's lapping
        into a stone turtle you'd see the white bread changing
        your wine within my tumbler like red blood rising,
        the eiderdown would dissolve into little blue flames
                                    in silence
        and the brittle-beaked mug splinter into swordgrass.
O mother, O mother, my own good mother
        my step may not sound in the paternal house,
I must live deep in the green wood's underbrush
        no room for my tangled antlers in your shadowy
house, no room in your yard for my cemetery
        antlers, for my foliated horns are a loud world-tree
their leaves displaced by stars, their green moss by the
                                    Milky Way.
        Sweet-scented herbs must I take in my mouth, only
the first-growth grasses can my spittle liquify,
        I may no longer drink from the flowered mug you bring
only from a clean spring, only from a clean spring!

I do not understand, do not understand your strange tortured
                                    words, my son
you speak like a stag, a stag's soul seems to possess you, my
                                    unfortunate one.
When the turtle-dove cries, the turtle-dove cries, when the little
                                    bird sings, the little bird sings,
                                    my son
wherefore am I – in the whole universe am I the last lost
                                    soul left, the only one?
Do you remember, do you remember your small once-young
                                    mother, my son?
I do not grasp, do not grasp your sad tortured words my long
                                    lost son.

Do you remember how you came running, running home to me
                                    so happy with your school report,

214

you dissected a bull-frog, spreading out on the fence his
freckled webbed paddle-feet,
and how you pored over the books on aircraft, how you followed
me in to help with the washing,
you were in love with Irene B., your best friend was V.J.,
and there was H.S., the wild orchid-bearded painter,
and do you remember on Saturday nights, when your father came
home sober, how happy you were?

O mother, my mother, do not speak of my sweetheart of old
or of my friend
like fish they fleet by in cold depths,
the vermilion-chinned painter
who knows now where he has gone his shouting way, who
knows mother, where my youth
has gone?
Mother, my mother, do not recall my father, out of his flesh
sorrow has sprouted,
sorrow blossoms from the dark earth, do not recall
my father, my father,
from the grave he'd rise, gathering about him his
yellowed bones,
from the grave stagger, hair and nails growing anew.
Oh! Oh! Uncle Wilhelm came, the coffin-maker, that
puppet-faced man,
he told us to take your feet and drop you neatly in the coffin.
I retched because I was afraid. I had come straight home
from Pest that day.
You too, my father, went back and forth to Pest, you were
only an office messenger. The
rails twisted up.
Oh, the stabbing knives in my belly then, shadows from the
candle ravined your tight cheeks,
your new son-in-law, Laci the barber, shaved you that day, the
candle dribbling the while like
a silent baby
regurgitating its glistening entrails, its long luminous nerves
like vines.
The choral society stood round you in their purple hats,
mourning you at the tops of
their voices,
with one finger I traced the rim of your forehead.
Your hair was alive still,

I heard it grow, I saw the bristles sprout from your chin
blackened by morning, the next day your throat had sunk
                        beneath snake-grass stalks of hair
its curve like a soft-furred cantaloup, the colour of a yellow
                        haired caterpillar upon blue
                        cabbage skin.
Oh, and I thought your hair, your beard, would overgrow
                        the whole room, the yard
the entire world, stars nestling like cells in its hiving strands.
Ah! Heavy green rain started then to fall, the team of red
                        horses before the hearse neighed
                        in terror,
one lashing out above your head with a lightning bolt hoof,
                        the other relentlessly pissing
so that his purple parts passed out with it like a hanged
                        man's tongue, while their
                        coachman cursed
and the downpour washed round the huddled brassbandsmen.
                        Then all those old friends blew
                        with a will
sobbing as they played, beside the globe-thistle studded
                        chapel wall,
those old friends blew till their lips swelled blue, and the tune
                        spiralled out and up,
the old friends blew with those cracked lips bleeding now,
                        with eyeballs staring,
blew for the card games and booze, the bloated, the withered
                        and the trumped women,
played you out for the red-letter day beer-money, the tips
                        sent whirling into space after you
they blew, sobbing as they blew sadly down into the
                        sedimentary layers of silted
                        sadness,
music pouring from the burnished mouths, from rings of brass
                        into putrescent nothingness,
out of it streamed the petrified sweethearts, rotting women,
                        and mouldy grandfathers in
                        the melody,
with small cottages, cradles, and rolling like onions a
                        generation of enamel-swollen,
                        silver-bodied watches,
Easter bells and multifarious saviours there came also on
                        wide-spreading wings of sound

that summoned up satchels, railway wheels, and soldiers
                    brass-buttoned at the salute,
the old friends played on, teeth reddening under lips curled
                    back and swollen like
                    blackened liver,
and yourself conducting the choir – Well done, boys, that's
                    grand, carry it on, don't stop now!
all the time, with hands clasped tight, those gold spiders with
                    huge legs knotted like spoke-
                    joints, resting on your heart,
in the cupboard your collapsed boots await the relations,
                    white socks naked on your
                    bread-crust curling feet,
old friends that day played you out in the crashing rain,
                    valves snapping like steel Adam's
                    apples
like fangs of antediluvian birds, teeth of the *Carcharodon*
                    looking for carrion from those
                    brass trumpets,
O mother, my mother, do not recall my father
let my father be, lest his eyes burst out of the
                    reopening earth.

Her own son the mother called
    from afar crying:
Come back, my own son, come back
    turn away from that stone-world
you stag of the stone-woods, the idustrialized air,
                    electric grids,
chemical lightenings, iron bridges, and streetcars lap up
                    your blood,
    day by day they make a hundred assaults on you,
                    yet you never hit back,
it is I calling you, your own mother
    come back, my own son, come back.

There he stood on the renewing crags of time,
stood on the ringed summit of the sublime
universe, there stood the lad at the gate of secrets,
his antler prongs were playing with the stars,
with a stag's voice down the world's lost paths
he called back to his life-giving mother:
    Mother, my mother, I cannot go back

pure gold seethes in my hundred wounds,
day by day, a hundred bullets knock me from my feet
and day by day I rise again, a hundred times more complete,
day by day I die three billion times,
day by day I'm born three billion times,
each prong of my antlers is a dual-based pylon,
each branch of my antlers a high-tension wire,
my eyes are ports for ocean-going merchantmen, my veins
                              are tarry cables, these
teeth are iron bridges, and in my heart the surge of
                              monster-infested seas,
each vertebra is a teeming metropolis, for a spleen I have a
                              smoke-puffing barge
each of my cells is a factory, my atoms are solar systems
sun and moon swing in my testicles, the Milky Way is
                              my bone marrow,
each point of space is one part of my body
my brain's impulse is out in the curling galaxies.

Lost son of mine, come back for all that – Oh, come back,
sleepless your mother's eyes shall watch on for you still.

Only to die will I return, only to die come back,
yes, I will come, will come to die
and when I have come – but to die – my mother
then may you lay me in the parental house,
with your marbled hand you may wash my body
and my glandulous eyelids close with a kiss.
    And then, when my flesh falls apart
and lies in its own stench, yet deep in flowers
    then shall I feed on your blood, be your body's fruit
then shall I be your own small son again,
and this shall give pain to you alone mother,
    to you alone, O my mother.

From the volume Harc a fehér báránnyal (Battling the white Lamb),
1957

English version by Kenneth McRobbie, with Ilona Duczyńska

Seasons

Sped is Autumn. And decay is sped.
I tore towards you across the rotting plants.
My helpless eyes hid behind the empty lids of the dead
as solitary naked crabs in pearl rimmed shells.
Dead men's shadows run purple from the whale-tooth
railings.
Mouldering babies hang from their maw, and moaning soiled
chrysanthemums.
A blue dove they led towards me, her little feet belled silver
chains trailing.
I slumped before your atom-splitting smile, turned grey under
your wandering glance.

And Winter's gone. Not like others we knew.
The city's jaw of bells gnaws the bald heavens.
My teeth machine-gun the cold streets where I begged
bread for you.
Winter ties up the woods in silence, knotting the white ends.
Hyacinth-blue the shadows from fairyland behind
that railing,
up to your silent window lope animals in a sorrowing throng.
Grey ruin hugging the lilac, at bedside I listen to your careless
babbling,
deer, hare and thrush in the marked snow follow your
flame-white song.

Woe to this Spring! Foam encrusts the walls
where organic green flesh has dried in a
cracked glaze,
shreds of dead flowers shrivel beside the spooled tendrils
death's whirling arms for the bright seed grains reaching
from outer space.
Shadows vomit up green bile beside the railing,
cannibal shark and saw-tooth starfish thrash hungry in swarms
as lust sprouts at your dribbled prayers, chuckles and
delighted gabbling.
I throw myself here, grass on living-grave, covering breasts
fragrant as tombs.

And in time Summer! Into a gold medal it
mints a people.

The moon's randy stallion flashes his badge with
a blue grin,
beneath ropes of nerves, cries of pain rise from the world.
In ultra-violet froth the insect slavers in its daydream.
Acid shadows are licking out from the snake-fang railing,
lizard fingers grasp at your bulging heart, where many moths to
red ash burned.
Under hardening leaves I still listen to your female flower's
husky sobbing,
groaning by the red cave's dripstone garden – great panther,
I, in your heart buried.

Written in Spring, 1957, his wife having been temporarily of unsound mind.

Kortárs (The Contemporary), *June, 1958.*

English version by Kenneth McRobbie

Appendix

NOTES ON THE AUTHORS

PART ONE

ZSIGMOND MÓRICZ (1879 – 1942). Móricz marks the beginning of the new writing in Hungary after the pale, idyllic literature of the late nineteenth century.

He was born in a small village east of the River Tisza. His father was a robust peasant, his mother a Calvinist minister's daughter, who was sensitive and refined.

Antal Szerb, the literary historian, assassinated by the Hungarian Nazis in 1944, sees a 'rhythmically interchanging duality' in his *oeuvre*. In Móricz' unequalled descriptions of the Hungarian peasant his style is expressionist, terse. His themes are land-hunger, brute force, class-feeling and stark passion. When he treats of his other theme, the gentry, the rural middle classes, the people in the small towns in the Plains, the tone mellows into minutely realistic detailing. Both themes are cast in the same tragic mould of the Magyar destiny, where 'boundless energies either turn to murderous passion, or, in frustration, give way to lethargy; for the Magyar scene is not wide enough to give play to the life-force of the race.'

Móricz was thirty when he was discovered as a writer by the literary periodical *Nyugat*, where his first short story, 'Seven pennies' appeared. He became co-editor of *Nyugat* in later years. His ample writings were the first in Hungary to combine high literary merit with a wide readership. He lived to see the rise, in the Thirties, of the young generation of Populist writers, who regarded him as their founder, and in them he recognized a hope for Hungary.

* * *

GYULA ILLYÉS was born in 1902 in Ráczegres, a Transdanubian *puszta*, the son of a paid-in-kind estate servant. There was no lower status in the social hierarchy of the poor in old Hungary. The fondest dream of every estate servant was to rise to poor peasant rank, and retire to the neighbouring village after his lifetime of servitude – an ambition that few achieved. The Illyés family, however, had some relatives in the nearby district town, where the gifted boy eventually was sent to school. Gyula Illyés went to the University in Budapest, and later in Paris, starving his way, as was customary with the have-not intelligentsia of East and Central Europe. His first poems appeared in 1926, revealing an earthbound poetic essence. Illyés never lost touch with his native self in the variations of his poetry between the idyllic and the heroic.

In the early 'Thirties Illyés dedicated himself to the cause that later was named Populist. His unique contribution to the village explorers' work, his largely autobiographical *People of the puszta* became a classic. His personal insight and verbal magic made painstaking sociological detail come to life. The English reader may find a parallel in W. H. Hudson's descriptions of the natural history of the primeval forest.

Illyés' probings into the dark recesses of servile existence place him among the writers of great confessions: his own soul is shown 'nimble in bending.' He put his finger on the symptom of mortification that a social stratum – his own – has suffered at the hands of history: dumb servility, impassively accepted as second nature.

Illyés remained foremost among the Populist writers. He took part in the setting up of the March Front in 1937, and its later political incarnation, the National Peasant Party. The Soviet sponsored land reform of 1945 brought the realization of his dreams. He adhered to the National Peasant Party until 1948, when it lost its identity under the new Communist dictatorship. After that he remained uncommitted. Generally recognized as the greatest living poet of Hungary, Illyés has attained the stature of a national poet in his heroic poetry, 'Hand of Hunyadi', 'Ode to Bartók,' and 'Of tyranny, in one breath.'

* * *

ÁRON TAMÁSI was born in 1898 in a small Transylvanian highland village into an abjectly poor peasant family. He is a Szekler by birth and by his almost mystical self-identification with the ethnic essence of his people. A Szekler is to the Magyars of Transylvania roughly what a Scots Highlander would be to a Scot of the Lowlands.

Tamási's short stories are the work of a creative moral personality, a humanist and a poet. The sentences are as if carved in seasoned hardwood. He uses few words, but captures from the spirit of the language a virginal spare beauty. His prose has its own intricate hidden rhythm. Tamási is a fount from which folk-myth spurts in ever new shapes and forms: the parable, unassuming anecdotes, the scurrilous tale, the pagan enchantment, the messianic heartbeat. None of the Populist writers made as direct an appeal to their readers' imagination as Tamási, and none were more highly regarded by friend and enemy. Tamási himself goes through life as if he had stepped out of one of his own fairy-tales.

The writer's natural commitment to intellectual honesty and integrity of artistic expression was Tamási's guide in the fighting years of the Populist movement under the Horthy era, in the first hopeful years after 1945, and during the dark years of the Rákosi régime and the direction of literature. It remained his guide in the writers' movement of 1956, in which he took a leading part. After the revolution was shattered, Tamási is assumed to have written the last statement of the writers' creed, dated December 16, 1956. One year later he published his own personal declaration of faith. Its dignity, assurance and inner clarity had an electrifying effect on the post-revolutionary public which in any case was turning with reviving interest towards the Populist classics.

* * *

PÁL SZABÓ was born in 1893 in a small village in Bihar county on the eastern fringe of the Great Plain. He too was the son of a peasant. His native village, its characters and destinies are drawn in his novel *The mills of God*. Among the Populist writers Szabó is the novelist rather than the sociographer as such. Politically, we find him in the ranks of the March Front and the National Peasant Party. In later years he showed himself amenable to the wishes and directives of the Rákosi régime. The distinctive personal quality of his writing gave way in *New soil* to the slick sentences and predictable events of 'socialist realism' – or tried to. He made a recovery in 1953, and his autobiography *The unquiet life* shows once more his own vibrant, jerky style.

* * *

PÉTER VERES was born in 1897 in one of the huge villages of the Great Plain, not far from Debreczen. These town-sized communities, Calvinist in creed, have populations of around 10,000 and are inhabited solely by peasants – rich, poor and destitute. Veres was born into a landless peasant family and by the time he was forty had waged the rural pauper's long struggle for survival as farm hand, casual labourer, sharecropper, petty tenant, harvester and pick-and-shovel man on the railway. Veres is the poor peasant incarnate. He was Head of the Commission for Land Distribution and twice Cabinet Minister after that. Yet he never changed his way of life.

Veres began to write in the early 'Thirties and the flowing ease of his style matched the wealth of his knowledge of the ways of animals, plants and men, of the seasons, the crops, weeds, tools, of neighbours, generations, feuds – a Hesiod in prose. In *Village chronicle* he wrote of the still remembered struggles of the revolutionary *agrarismo* in his native Balmazujváros, the successive generations of village leaders and the movements that were altogether off the beaten track and found their vehicles in the extremist religious sects. Everything he wrote – sociographies, pamphlets, recollections, newspaper articles and later on, stories and novels have a genuine ring. Veres' committedness is to his class, the destitute, hard-working peasantry. In drawing them he is wily and wise, humorous and human. His peasant roots are also the roots of his inner independence.

When, in the later 'Thirties, the Populist writers came to be the political representatives of the poor peasantry, Veres became a prominent leader in the National Peasant Party. After ten years of eminence in public life he was deposed as Minister of Defence and ousted from the political scene in the Summer of 1948 by the newly established Communist dictatorship, owing to a disagreement in agricultural policy. Veres' book *The Peasant Future* in which he outlined a picture of post-land reform peasant economies appeared almost exactly at the same time as Rákosi's announcement of a policy of collectivization in agriculture. Veres went home to his plough and his pen with the sardonic remark: 'I have been appointed a great writer.'

* * *

TIBOR DÉRY was born in 1894 in Budapest, the son of a wealthy manufacturer. Déry led a sheltered life until he entered the flourishing family business. As a child a serious illness kept him even more remote from the world than the social *milieu* warranted. Illness, childhood and youth were past before that remoteness began to wear off. Some remnant of it later, in his mature years, may have been at the core of his unbending strength in resisting evil.

Young Déry, heir apparent to the Nasici timber empire as its Director's nephew, entered the saw-mill at twenty-two in a suitably humble position to learn the trade. In six years he learned a great deal about the life of the workers. Meanwhile Déry was already a young writer of promise, whose surrealist stories appeared in the periodical *Nyugat*. He was well read in the Russian classics and in socialist theory. The times were stormy. In 1918 he brought out the saw-mill workers on strike, and they all joined the social democratic trade union. Soon after the founding of the Hungarian Communist Party at the end of 1918 Déry joined it. His life and work in the next fifteen years were unsettled, whether he happened to be in exile or at home. Hitler's access to power brought the final change, as Déry put it turning 'rebel into revolutionary.' He began work on his novel *The unfinished sentence*, which could not appear under the Horthy régime and was published only after 1945. Of his second novel, *Response*, the life of a worker planned as a trilogy, only two parts appeared – the response to existence given by childhood, and the response given by adolescence. The response of manhood remains unwritten, at least by the pen. The hero of Déry's book is a young working lad who does not find the solutions to his problems ready-made. The first volume made a deep impression and touched off a heated controversy in the country. The trend was already towards direction in literature and 'socialist realism.' Déry, partially swayed by his critics, lost originality in the second volume. He grew to full stature in 1956. Revulsion at the crimes of the Rákosi régime inspired his novel *Niki, the story of a dog*, and the short story published here under the title *Odysseus*.

As a leader in the writers' fight for free artistic expression, and in their fight against the conditions created by tryannical misgovernment, Déry was uncompromising, and after the Revolution he was sentenced to nine years imprisonment. He was released in Spring 1960.

His intimate knowledge of the industrial workers' lives ensures him a place in the portrayal of the world of factory and plant which is not far removed from the place the Populist writers hold in the exploration of the village.

* * *

LÁSZLÓ NÉMETH was born in 1901, in a Transdanubian village. A leader of men, social philosopher, utopian thinker, literary critic – he made his mark from the start on the somewhat diffuse movement of the village explorers and Populist writers. As far as the current classification of Left, Right and Centre is applicable to that movement he can be said to have constituted the Centre. Of Protestant stock and persuasion, and with a certain conservative bent, his preoccupation with the racial values of his people never lacked independence and critical balance. During the 'Thirties he edited, and wrote single-handed a periodical, *Tanu (Witness)* – truly a cultural and sociophilosophical documentary of the period. Half-hidden by his profound erudition, Németh the playwright and novelist was steadily moving to the front rank of Hungarian writers.

György Lukács, the Marxist philosopher and literary critic recognized his genius and did much to advance Németh's work. As long as his protection availed, that is, up to 1948, Németh's work continued to be printed, though under attack. In that year he completed his masterpiece, the monumental novel *Égető Eszter*, but it was to be nine more years before it left the printing press, in 1957. Here he paints on a broad canvas. In the microcosm of a small rural town in the Plains, in the veiled depths of personal existence, his heroine's life unfolds from early childhood to middle age; so does the century's from its birth to the half-way mark – from calm to apocalypse. Németh draws detail with infinite love and precision: every phrase comes alive. Németh, the non-Communist experienced no inner compulsion to modify his art, as did Déry the Communist or Pál Szabó the sympathizer. His life-size vision of the random texture of events would not adjust to imposed norms. In 1948 Németh went into dogged, but productive silence. Out of this withdrawal issued the cycle of Historical plays, each built round the figure of a tragic seeker – John Hus, Joseph II, Scéchenyi, Petőfi and Galileo, whose poignant self-accusation brought the image of a nation on to the stage.

Németh's works were widely published in the months preceding and following the October Revolution. Beside two volumes of historical plays two volumes of social drama appeared, written in the years of struggle against the Horthy régime. Here his weird crew of home-grown, countryside utopians nurse their dreams and go to their doom.

Part Two

ATTILA JÓZSEF (1905 – 1937) was born into the poorest pro-
letariat of Budapest. His father went off to America, leaving his
wife destitute and three small children. At the age of three Attila
and a sister were farmed out in a village, while the mother worked
in Budapest as a washerwoman. The boy worked for his keep before
he was seven, minding geese and pigs. Back with his mother, he
sold matches in the street, or buns, books even –

> Colporteur qui sans les lire cherche à vendre
> Móricz et Shaw, Zola, Cocteau, Barbusse . . .
>
> Marchand maigre de croissants d'or
> J'en vois manger et ne les mange
>
> Je n'ai ni lard ni feu. Je dors
> Sur les bancs et l'herbe des anges.[1]

Taking on odd jobs, Attila worked his way through a provincial
high school, not without coming into conflict with authority, for
he published poems in the local newspaper which were considered
blasphemy and treason. He was discovered by the literary critics of
the periodical *Nyugat* early in life. After finishing high school he
went to Paris and studied at the Sorbonne for a year, in that abject
poverty in which he spent every year of his short life. His thought
matured on Hegel and Marx, still vibrating from his close touch
with the French avant-garde Attila returned to Budapest at the
high tide of his creative power. He joined the underground workers'
movement. Immortal verse now began to appear in clandestine
mimeographed sheets of the Communist youth.

That the union did not last, goes almost without saying. Like
so many before and after, he was hounded from the Communist
ranks by narrow-minded doctrinaires. Like so few, he never lost
his *Weltanschauung*, remaining at one with the movement in the
broad, historical sense. Attila József lived in a world warped by
the ghastly realities of fascism. His socialist faith was healthy and
potent, a heady tonic. The bitter antinomies of its realization
in the living body of society were to face another generation of
poets.

[1] From the French version by Jean Cocteau of Attila József's poem. In *Hommage
à Attila József par les poètes français* (Seghers), 1955.

Burning away fast in the creative fires of his mind, Attila József was sombre and lonely in his later years. Shiftless, dreading the final grip of insanity, he died, hurling himself under the wheels of a goods train. He was thirty-two.

Attila József created an epoch in Hungarian lyric poetry, as Ady did before him. He was a poet of the universal human world, of the poor, of God and history, the city slums and the fields. In this synthesis there was a populism wholly his own, in which his poetic style was rooted with its 'peculiar union of folk-realism, symbolist poignancy, and the surrealist's search for psychological validity'.[2]

For posterity Attila József remains the lonely giant, Bartók's poet brother. Sparsely read in the Zhdanov era, he remained the aloof stranger – revered, but not followed, even in the time of the revolt against it. Only in the youngest generation of poets, tempered by the adversities that fate and faith may bring, is a kindred strain discernible – in Ferenc Juhász and some of his contemporaries.

* * *

The Communist Poets

LÁSZLÓ BENJÁMIN was born in 1915, in a workers' district of Budapest, where he grew up in poverty. After 1945 he took part in political activities, with little success. He was interested in poetry and in poetry only. After 1948 he came into his own. Zhdanov notwithstanding, his poems had strength, depth and simplicity. The turning-point in his life came in 1953, with Imre Nagy's accession to premiership. Recognition of the state of affairs within party and country was beginning to spread. Benjámin became a fighter for the reform of the party. In discussion he was blunt, even coarse. A powerful heart and mind, he was to suffer the agonies of his involvement in guilt, for he had turned against his closest friend, the writer Sándor Haraszti, one of the sterling characters who will always stand up against iniquity and evil. Accused of treason along with László Rajk in the political frame-up, Haraszti was condemned to death and kept indefinitely in the condemned cell. Benjámin, in his naiveté, had believed the charges

[2] From a recent study on the poet by József Révai.

against him to be true. One of his poems gave voice to the tragic involvement, not of the two friends only, but of a whole generation:

> Let us wrench the ideal free – we staked our lives
> on it – from the mire, together we'll heave and claw
> with our bare nails until we lift it high
> in all its purity, for the world to see.
> May it redeem me too. Dishonoured, I
> will yet strive on to reach the unattainable,
> to remedy the irremediable.

ZOLTÁN ZELK was born in 1906, in a small place to the east of Debreczen, Érmihályfalva. His father was a cantor in the synagogue, and the home *milieu* was that of the Jewish lower middle class of the countryside, neither rural nor urban, It was charged with sentiment. As a boy Zelk was a grocer's assistant in a neighbouring town, and joined the labour youth. His poems appeared in the social democratic press, and soon in the *Nyugat*. In 1945 he became a Communist, and from 1948 onwards a poet – and only a poet. That was a year of decision for many intellectuals of the Left. Zelk conformed to the party line and to the party's needs out of profound conviction. He wrote remarkable poetry in that period. In later years he publicly renounced his odes to Stalin and to Rákosi. In opposition he hit harder than anyone; in debate he was like one possessed – a flaming orator. Haunted by fear – and worse, by fear of cowardice, Zelk in the course of events was maltreated in jail. His new poems appeared in 1962, several years after his release.

LAJOS TAMÁSI, born in 1923 in a small village of Transdanubia not far from Illyés' birthplace, was the son of a casual labourer. Living in stark poverty, he went through high school amid many privations. In 1945 he joined the Communist Party. Tamási was the ideal image of the young worker, active, forthright and amiable. He was soon entrusted with a function in the Writers' Association which entailed the high responsibility of conscientiously representing the party's line and interests among the writers. Speaking his mind fearlessly, Tamási himself became a leader in the writers' fight for freedom of criticism. His earlier poetry had been hardly significant. His own search for the Communist's downright answer to stark, fundamental doubts gave his poems a new quality and power. He published again in 1962.

PÉTER KUCZKA was born in 1923 at the old Transdanubian city of Székesfehérvár, of middle-class parents. A convert to Communism, his adherence to the Party was of passionate intensity. In his earlier poetry, which was not unimpressive, he was in form and substance a disciple of Mayakovsky. He was hot-headed and impetuous in those years of unbounded allegiance. Later, when awareness of the country's condition hit him, a meditative mood prevailed. Soberly taking stock, Kuczka, in 1953 was the first among Communist poets to voice the people's sufferings and to warn the party of the dangers of enforcing dogmatic policies in a long poetic recording, 'North-eastern diary'. It was an exemplary act of courage.

* * *

FERENC JUHÁSZ the youngest poet in this selection, was born in 1928 in a small village in Transdanubia, not very far from Budapest. He was a peasant boy, and only 17 years old when the new régime began, in 1945. Hence Juhász and his generation are as native-born to the socialist world. The poets Laszló Nagy and István Simon were his friends. Juhász had a strong apolitical leaning, both in regard to official and oppositional activities. His conscious life began in the infancy of the new epoch; he was not a convert, nor did he become an apostate.

He turned into a poet at nineteen. Up to that time, at least as he put it, he only wrote random lines that did not link up. Of these he had in the end two suitcases full, and burnt them when he was admitted, in 1947, to the People's College named after Attila József. Here he fell in love with a peasant-girl student, Erzsébet Szeverényi, 'when I first saw her standing on top of the staircase, as I entered the College diffidently, carrying my humble belongings'. They married soon after. Juhász started out in life, a poet. Their union was the supreme reality – in their fields of bliss and later, in the desolation of her temporary derangement.

What Juhász is as a poet, he was from the start. But the world of perception and the landscape of the mind formed visions in time almost beyond human endurance.

In his early years he lived and wrote in full harmony with the world in transformation around him. In this period his poetry was none the worse for being 'socialist realist,' in his own naive, broad interpretation. His poetic mood changed freely from the idyllic to the hilarious in a satirical village epic, *The frost-flower's cockerel*, which made riotious fun of the characters on a new collective farm. No one in 1951 had dared touch on such a subject, but Juhász disarmed his critics by the sheer beauty of the epic and his unquenchable personality.

If there is a recurrence of populism in Juhász, it is populism with a difference: his native world is a strange compound of nature, folk-tale and technology. These are also the media of his thought and philosophy. Modern technology is here absorbed and transcended – Juhász is building a place for it in original nature and original man. This, in his reading is socialism.

Releasing a wholly novel wealth of lyric imagery in his myth-creating folk-tale poems, Juhász made the final turn off the approved track.

An expanded universe of the senses, biological visions, macrocosmic phantasy blended in torrents of images of universal human validity with the later tragic turn of his personal life. It is for the future literary historian to write his story. We have but the apocalyptic witness of his poetry in the last published volume, *Battling the White Lamb*, and the two poems published in 1958, 'Swan-fate of our love' and 'Seasons'. After another break of four years he now publishes again.